D0712600

King Philip's War

THE CONFLICT OVER
NEW ENGLAND

LANDMARK EVENTS IN NATIVE AMERICAN HISTORY

THE APACHE WARS
The Final Resistance

BLACK HAWK AND THE WAR OF 1832
Removal in the North

CODE TALKERS AND WARRIORS
Native Americans and World War II

KING PHILIP'S WAR
The Conflict Over New England

LITTLE BIGHORN
Winning the Battle, Losing the War

THE LONG WALK
The Forced Navajo Exile

RED POWER
The Native American Civil Rights Movement

THE TRAIL OF TEARS
Removal in the South

King Philip's War

THE CONFLICT OVER NEW ENGLAND

DANIEL R. MANDELL

Associate Professor of History
Truman State University

SERIES EDITOR: PAUL C. ROSIER

Assistant Professor of History
Villanova University

CHELSEA HOUSE
PUBLISHERS
An imprint of Infobase Publishing

For David and Joshua,
in the hope that someday they will find it enjoyable and useful.

Cover: An artist's rendition of the attack on Deerfield, Massachusetts, during King Philip's War.

KING PHILIP'S WAR: The Conflict Over New England

Chelsea House
An imprint of Infobase Publishing
132 West 31st Street
New York NY 10001

Library of Congress Cataloging-in-Publication Data
Mandell, Daniel R., 1956–
King Philip's war : the conflict over New England / Daniel R. Mandell.
     p. cm.—(Landmark events in Native American history)
Includes bibliographical references and index.
ISBN-13: 978-0-7910-9346-7 (hardcover)
ISBN-10: 0-7910-9346-8 (hardcover)
1. King Philip's War, 1675–1676   2. Wampanoag Indians—Wars
3. New England—History—Colonial period, ca. 1600–1775.
I. Title.   II. Series.
E83.67.M33 2007
973.2'4—dc22   2006102258

Chelsea House books are available at special discounts when purchased in bulk quantities for businesses, associations, institutions, or sales promotions. Please call our Special Sales Department in New York at (212) 967–8800 or (800) 322–8755.

You can find Chelsea House on the World Wide Web at
http://www.chelseahouse.com

Series design by Erika K. Arroyo
Cover design by Ben Peterson
Illustrations by Sholto Ainslie

Printed in the United States of America
Bang NMSG 10 9 8 7 6 5 4 3 2 1

This book is printed on acid-free paper.

All links and Web addresses were checked and verified to be correct at the time of publication. Because of the dynamic nature of the Web, some addresses and links may have changed since publication and may no longer be valid.

Contents

Endings and Beginnings, 1620–1635

IN MID-JUNE 1675, ON A SMALL ISLAND IN NARRAGANSETT Bay, the 35-year-old sachem (leader) of the Wampanoags, named Philip by the English and Metacom by his people, sat "veri friendly" with the deputy governor of the English colony of Rhode Island, John Easton. But the circumstances of their meeting were far from peaceful, and they were not alone: Metacom had 40 of his warriors with him, all armed. For more than a decade, the English colonists in Plymouth had been pressuring the Wampanoag sachem, in order to reduce his sovereignty and gain control of his land. Plymouth Colony had violated the 1621 agreement with Metacom's father, Massasoit, purchased land from individual Indians without the sachem's approval, and, with the support of the newer colonies of Massachusetts and Connecticut, forced the Native American leader to publicly announce that he was a subject of the colony's government instead of a sovereign equal. The anger and frustration of Metacom and his Wampanoag warriors had been apparent for months.

Nor were the Wampanoags alone in their resentment. The Narragansett, Nipmuc, Pequot, and other tribes had also experienced significant changes since that handful of Englishmen met Massasoit in 1621. The colonists had become more powerful and confident and began to spread throughout the region, outnumbering the Indians and rearranging the

Metacom, or King Philip, was the sachem (leader) of the Wampanoags from 1662 until his death in 1676. This illustration is an artist's representation; Metacom's image was never captured during his lifetime.

political landscape through treaties, alliances, and war. Their farms had even reshaped the land. Now the English feared and anticipated that a violent response would soon come, and reports pointed to efforts by Metacom to forge an alliance with other tribes in the region. The colonists of Rhode Island had maintained very good relations with the Indians, and Easton, along with four other Rhode Islanders, sought a meeting with Metacom to prevent the conflict from escalating into war.

At the meeting, Metacom and his men complained that the English had caused the problems. When Easton suggested arbitration, they complained that the colonists frequently used English arbitrators to unfairly take Native American lands. Easton suggested two unbiased judges, a sachem and New York governor Edward Andros, and the Wampanoags seemed interested. Metacom then insisted on airing their grievances.

When the English had first arrived in the area, Massasoit, the Wampanoag sachem, kept other tribes from harming the small, weak party of Pilgrims; now, Metacom said, Massasoit's heirs were being poorly repaid. In 1660, Metacom's brother had been forced at gunpoint to travel to Plymouth Colony and had died on the journey, apparently poisoned.

In regard to more general problems, Metacom charged that, when disputes arose, the English believed Indians only when it suited them, and then chose to believe those who lied or cheated. When a sachem sold land, the colonists always claimed more. Traders sold Indians rum and then cheated them of land when they became drunk; and the addicted Native Americans preyed on the sober to feed their habit. The English violated native customs by manipulating the selection of sachems. And growing numbers of English cattle and horses wandered onto Native American cornfields and destroyed their crops.

Easton and his colleagues listened, but, reluctant to judge, responded only by telling the Indians that they should not fight the English, who had grown strong in their ever-increasing numbers. The Wampanoags agreed in principle, but insisted that the colonists must be as fair to them as the strong Massasoit had been to that first weak group of English settlers.

The leaders of Plymouth at the time, however, rejected Easton's effort at mediation. One week later, angry Wampanoag warriors appeared with their muskets on the edge of Swansea, a town built on tribal land without Metacom's approval. After an English boy shot a warrior, the rest attacked the settlement and an all-out war began. During the following few months, the war engulfed the entire region, involving every tribe, colony, and village. Some Indians fought for the English but most took the field against the colonists, largely because throughout the previous half-century they had experienced the same problems that Metacom had complained about to Easton.

At first the English seemed helpless and incompetent. They were unable to stop Metacom from raiding their towns and gaining the support of other tribes to the north and west. The colonists abandoned villages inland and streamed into Boston. But gradually the English gained the advantage, learning from their mistakes, marshalling their Native American allies (particularly the Mohawks) and more effectively using their superior numbers and resources. A terrible winter and the extended conflict cut off the food supplies needed by the Indian warriors and families, who had left their villages either to fight the English or from fear of the colonists. By late spring 1676, many Native Americans were starving and their alliance was in tatters. Metacom retreated with some of the few remaining Wampanoag warriors to seek refuge in his home territory.

As the uprising dissolved, a squad, including many of the sachem's former supporters, began hunting the man who was both the trigger and the symbol of the war. They captured Metacom's wife and son, and the colonial authorities apparently sold the two into slavery in the West Indies, like most of the captured Indians. On August 12, 1676, Metacom was shot by an Indian serving with a scouting party led by an Englishman. His body was cut up and the pieces were distributed among the colonies. Some time later his head disappeared from the spike outside Plymouth. A Wampanoag legend holds that Metacom's warriors stole his head and secretly buried it near Mount Hope (now Bristol, Rhode Island), where his spirit still periodically speaks. King Philip's War decimated the Native American population in southern New England and, although many Indian communities remained in the region, they lacked the autonomy held before the war. At the same time, the colonists also suffered high casualties and did not return to abandoned towns for several decades. Although the regional conflict that resulted in the war had developed during the half-century since the English had arrived, the colonists' defeat of the Native American fight for independence marked a watershed in American history.

THE ARRIVAL OF THE EUROPEANS

The initial meetings between Native Americans and Europeans in southern New England were occasional encounters with explorers, such as Giovanni da Verrazzano in 1542, Samuel Champlain in 1604 and 1605, and John Smith in 1614. These encounters had unforeseen but very important effects on Native American groups. Social and political networks were reshaped among villages and tribes in New England; some leaders were able to increase their authority, while others lost prestige or faced raids by other groups seeking resources for trade with the Europeans. More significantly, from 1617 through 1618, an epidemic brought by Europeans killed a huge percentage of coastal Indians from southern Maine to Narragansett Bay. Among those most affected were the Patuxets (a subgroup within the Wampa-noag tribe) who lived along the bay that Smith had named Plymouth: many died, perhaps as much as 90 percent of the tribe, and many villages were completely decimated or abandoned by the few survivors. It was at the site of a Patuxet

CONFERENCE AND AGREEMENT BETWEEN PLYMOUTH COLONY AND MASSASOIT

The September 21, 1621, agreement between the English and Native Americans in the region that became known as southern New England was the first between the two groups. The Wampanoag sachem Massasoit hesitated before making contact with the English Separatists (Pilgrims) who had occupied an abandoned Patuxet village and renamed it Plymouth. But his people had been decimated by an epidemic (probably brought by European traders) and were now hard pressed by the Narragansetts, so he saw an unusual opportunity in creating an alliance with the newcomers. The English colonists, on the other hand, probably saw the resulting agreement as Massasoit's submission to English jurisdiction. The colonists clearly gained the power to decide disputes between individuals from the two groups and obtained support under English law for their colony.

After salutations, our Governour [William Bradford] kissing his hand, the King [Massasoit] kissed him, and so they sat downe. The Governour called for some strong water, and drunke to him, and he drunke a great draught that made him sweate all the while after. He called for a little fresh meate, which the King did eate willingly; and did give his followers. Then they treated of Peace, which was:

1. That neyther he nor any of his should injure or doe hurt to any of our people.

village that the first boatload of English colonists decided to settle.

These colonists, now generally known as Pilgrims, were better known at the time as Separatists: that is, they saw the Church of England as hopelessly corrupt and so they sought to

2. And if any of his did hurt to any of ours, he should send the offender, that we might punish him.

3. That if any of our Tooles were taken away when our people were at worke, he should cause them to be restored, and if ours did any harme to any of his, wee would doe the like to them.

4. If any did unjustly warre against him, we would ayde him; If any did warre against us, he should ayde us.

5. He should send to his neighbour Confederates, to certifie them of this, that they might not wrong us, but might be likewise comprised in the conditions of Peace.

6. That when their men came to us, they should leave their Bowes and Arrowes behind them, as wee should doe our Peeces when we came to them.

Lastly, that doing thus, King JAMES would esteeme of him as his friend and Alie: all which the King seemed to like well, and it was applauded of his followers . . . In his Attyre little or nothing differing from the rest of his followers, only in a great Chaine of white bone Beades about his necke, and at it behinde his necke, hangs a little bagg of Tobacco, which he dranke and gave us to drinke; his face was paynted with a sad red like murry, and oyled both head and face, that hee looked greasily . . . after all was done, the Governour conducted him to the Brooke, and there they embraced each other and he departed.[*]

---

[*] Anonymous, *A Relation [Mourt's Relation] or Journal of the Beginnings and Proceedings of the English Plantation Settled at Plimoth in New England* (London: John Bellamie, 1622), 32.

On September 21, 1621, the Wampanoags and English signed a treaty that ensured peace between the two groups. Massasoit, who is depicted in this engraving holding a pipe, hoped the alliance would help the Wampanoags in their feud with the Narragansetts.

create their own completely separate church and community—which, given the social and political norms of the period, meant they had to flee England to avoid whippings, fines, and worse. Some came from their temporary refuge in the Netherlands, while others came directly from England. Their advance party made landing at Nauset on Cape Cod in November 1620, but moved across the bay to Plymouth after encountering hostility from Native Americans. While the fields were largely cleared thanks to the work of the Patuxets, the Separatists had few supplies and knew little about the area, so many died during the winter.

The tribe nearest Plymouth, the Wampanoag, hesitated before making contact with the newcomers. They held a three-day gathering in the spring, no doubt to discuss their strategy toward the newcomers. Two representatives, Samoset (a visiting Wabanaki) and Squanto (a Patuxet who had been kidnapped, taken to Spain, and then reached England before returning), were dispatched to contact the English. The colonists had come in families rather than singly as young seamen, and seemed friendly and rather helpless, so the two envoys arranged a meeting between the Pilgrims and the Wampanoag sachem, Massasoit. The resulting agreement on September 21, 1621, (see sidebar on pages 12–13) can be viewed as either an alliance or a submission. Massasoit saw it as an alliance with the English newcomers, one that would give him new clout in his ongoing struggles with the Narragansetts and extend his endangered authority in the region. The English colonists, on the other hand, probably saw the agreement as one in which Massasoit consented to become a vassal of King James, and therefore put his land and people under English jurisdiction—although that did not mean that his people were subjects of Plymouth Colony. But the colonists clearly did gain the power to judge controversies between individuals from the two groups. They also gained vital support under English law for their colony, which had no charter from the king to create a new or distinct settlement.

Because they had no charter, the Plymouth colonists also felt the need to establish direct treaty relationships outside their connection with the Wampanoag sachem, and to sign treaties with nearby villages that were nominally subject to Massasoit's authority. That need became acute when Corbitant, a sachem of a village north of Plymouth, created an alliance with the Narragansetts and rallied Native American leaders who were alarmed at Massasoit's treaty with the colonists. When Squanto and Hobbamock (a Wampanoag leader who had become a trusted advisor to the Plymouth settlers) investigated, they were seized by Corbitant's warriors. Hobbamock escaped and obtained the help of the colonists. The Plymouth colonists then wrote a treaty in which a number of sachems swore allegiance to King James of England. A Plymouth contingent sailed a few days later for Massachusetts Bay, where they established cordial relations with Pawtucket and Massachusett villages. The English also returned the Narragansett's diplomatic challenge (a snakeskin) with an insult (filling it with musket shot). The English and Wampanoags finished the year with a shared harvest festival—the famous first Thanksgiving—that was a tradition among both peoples.

Other English settlers soon joined the Separatists in the region. Initially, fishermen and adventurers created only a few small outposts. In 1622, London merchant Thomas Weston sent 60 men to establish the second English settlement at Wessagussett, north of Plymouth, among the Massachusetts. However, the Wessagussett settlers proved unable to provide for themselves; the settlement lacked strong leadership or purpose, factions emerged, and starvation threatened. While some managed to live with the Native Americans, others stole their corn. In anger, the local sachem Pecksuot confronted the settlers. "Some of you steal our corn," he told them, "and I have sent you word times without number & yet our corn is stolen." When they tried to blame one individual, beating him and offering him to Pecksuot for more punishment, the sachem rejected the sacrifice and angrily charged that "you all steal my corn."[1] Such theft was indeed common among some early settlers unable to trade for or grow food. One of the Englishmen, Phineas Pratt, feared that the Indians would seek retribution and so he fled for Plymouth, staggering into town after wandering in the woods all night. Massasoit had already persuaded the Separatists to consider a preemptive strike against a supposed uprising. Pratt's description of events seemed to confirm the plot and the need to take action. The Massachusett sachems were invited into a meeting and then killed without warning. Wessagussett was abandoned.

A FLOOD OF PURITANS

Truly significant changes to the region came with the "Great Migration" of English Puritans to Massachusetts Bay Colony, north of Plymouth, beginning in 1630. Their leaders felt little need to formalize relations with the Native Americans. The Puritans held a charter from King Charles (bringing the document with them as a way of preventing the Crown from easily annulling it) and encountered only a few scattered, weak native villages along the bay. At the same time, these colonists knew it was important to create and maintain good relations with the Indians, who saw the newcomers as dangerous but potentially useful. During the first year of English settlement at Boston (formerly Shawmut), Bay Colony governor John Winthrop hosted leaders of villages and tribes from throughout the region. No treaties were signed with the leaders of nearby villages; instead, the rulers of the Bay Colony used laws and judicial rulings to manage relations. Their initial desire to focus on the immediate needs of settlement showed in their rejection of an offer by a Tunxis sachem to have them establish a fur trading post at his village along the Connecticut River.

The newcomers played a significant diplomatic role in the region, beginning with Massasoit's treaty with Plymouth against the Narragansetts. The large wave of English emigration extended the colonists' power and significance, and Native American leaders lined up to meet with Winthrop. In August 1631, Winthrop became the peacemaker between the Pennacooks and Wabanakis north of Boston in negotiating the release of the wife of a sachem who had been captured in a raid. In April 1632, Plymouth again became involved in the conflict between Massasoit and the Narragansetts. Two years later, theologian Roger Williams, who arrived in Massachusetts in 1630, played a major role in negotiating a peace between the two tribes. These diplomatic encounters would become even more significant as the brewing conflict around the Thames and Connecticut rivers resulted in war between the English and the Pequots.

As more English arrived in Massachusetts Bay Colony, new towns were founded north, south, and west of Boston. Founders of these new towns obtained grants of land and official status from the Massachusetts assembly of delegates, known as the General Court; the colonists did not, however, see the need to obtain grants from the Indians living on that land. But various factors, including challenges by Roger Williams, other colonial competitors, and the ire of English officials, led the colony's leaders to make formal purchases from Native American leaders. In 1632, they also became concerned that Native American anger at English expansion might drive an attack against Boston. Although an eruption of smallpox among the Indians the next year destroyed any potential opposition, Massachusetts would often make formal land purchases from sachems in order to avoid conflicts.

Openings to even more extensive settlements were provided by long-standing competition for access to European traders along Long Island Sound. In 1633, the Tunxis sachem again approached the English, this time in Plymouth, to establish a trading post in his territory that would allow him to compete with the Pequots for the Dutch trade. One year later, the Narragansetts gave land to Roger Williams just before he was driven out of Massachusetts Bay Colony due to his religious beliefs. He and others founded a new colony bordering on Wampanoag lands and Plymouth and Massachusetts, which became Rhode Island and Providence plantations. These religious and political dissidents sometimes found it important to gain recognition from both tribes for their settlements. Farther west, English colonists took advantage of the upheaval over the fur trade to obtain lands far up the Connecticut River. In July 1636, for example, Massachusetts Bay Colony official William Pynchon and others obtained a deed from the Agawam sachem for land that would become Springfield, for decades Massachusetts's western outpost. Such land negotiations became an important instrument and focus of Native American as well as English diplomacy. This was particularly true in the wake of the Pequot War as various groups of colonists and Indians maneuvered for survival and advantage. It would also be one of the primary causes of King Philip's War.

The Pequot War

NATIVE AMERICAN GROUPS IN SOUTHERN NEW ENGLAND found that the growing English presence created new opportunities as well as challenges. The 1633 smallpox epidemic decimated coastal and river Indian villages but left the Narragansetts relatively undisturbed, allowing them to join with Dutch traders to dominate the fur trade. The Pequots, concerned about losing their access to furs, tried to strike at the resulting Dutch–Narragansett trade axis, but succeeded only in angering both and losing their chief sachem to a Dutch raid. In desperation, Sassacus, the new Pequot sachem, approached Massachusetts Bay Colony officials for help and offered them a permanent trading post along the Connecticut River in exchange for helping arrange a truce with the Narragansetts. Massachusetts Bay Colony officials agreed to arrange the truce, but instead of the trading post asked for and received tribute and title to the whole Connecticut Valley. They also demanded the individuals suspected of killing English sea captain John Stone and his crew (see sidebar on pages 21–22).

MEETING BETWEEN PEQUOTS AND PURITAN EXPEDITION

In 1633, after the Puritans began settling Massachusetts, a smallpox epidemic decimated coastal and river tribes but left the Narragansetts relatively unaffected and preserved their position as the primary traders with the Dutch. The Pequots tried to drive out the Narragansetts and regain dominance but were badly defeated. They then approached the colonists of Massachusetts and offered them a trading post along the Connecticut River in exchange for help in arranging a truce with the Narragansetts. The colonial officials agreed, but instead of a trading post asked for and received tribute and title to the whole Connecticut Valley. English settlements quickly sprouted up in the area and the Pequots began to feel besieged within their territory. When English trader John Oldham was found murdered on his ship near Block Island, the Narragansetts were the obvious suspects, but that tribe's leaders managed to cast blame on the Pequots and promised to seek revenge for the English. In August 1636, Massachusetts dispatched a force to obtain satisfaction for Oldham and John Stone, an English sea captain murdered in 1634.

The next morning [the Pequots] sent early aboard an Ambassadour, a grave Senior, a man of good understanding, portly, cariage grave, and majesticall in his expressions; he demanded of us what the end of our comming was, to which we answered, that the Governours of the Bay sent us to demand the heads of those persons that had slaine Captaine Norton, and Captaine Stone, and the rest of their company, and that it was not the custome of the English to suffer murtherers to live, and therefore if they desired their owne peace and welfare, they will peaceably answer our expectation, and give us the heads of the murderers.

(continues)

(continued)

They being a witty and ingenious Nation, their Ambassadour laboured to excuse the matter, and answered, we know not that any of ours have slaine any English . . . we distinguish not betweene the Dutch and English, but tooke them to be one Nation, and therefore we doe not conceive that we wronged you, for [the Dutch] slew our king; and thinking these Captaines to be of the same Nation and people, as those that slew him, made us set upon this course of revenge. [The English refused to accept this reason, landed their forces, and confronted the Pequots. Their sachem then proposed a meeting after laying down their weapons.] But wee seeing their drift was to get our Armes, we rather chose to beat up the Drum and bid them battell, marching into a champion field we displayed our colours, but none would come neere us, but standing remotely off did laugh at us for our patience, wee suddenly set upon our march, and gave fire to as many as we could come neere, firing their Wigwams, spoyling their corn, and many other necessaries that they had buried in the ground we raked up, which the souldiers had for bootie. Thus we spent the day burning and spoyling the Countrey.[*]

---

[*] John Underhill, *Newes From America: Or, A New and Experimentall Discoverie of New England* (London: Peter Cole, 1638), 9–15.

The imposed agreement became one of the major steps along the road to the Pequot War, as English settlements were built along the Connecticut River and the Pequots' land was taken from them. The leaders of that tribe found their situation increasingly tenuous as they tried to compete with the Narragansetts, maintain the allegiance of outlying villages, and meet the continued English demands to turn over Stone's murderers. Sassacus began to lose power as some of his sachems, such as Wequash, began to strike out on their own and seek new alliances with the English. Some even joined with Uncas and his Mohegans, who were closely allied with leaders of the newly established Connecticut Colony and wanted Sassacus's power. (Uncas was a Pequot by birth but had rebelled against Sassacus and was expelled from the tribe.) In early 1636, a group of English investors built Fort Saybrook at the mouth of the Connecticut River,

After fleeing Plymouth Colony in 1636, Roger Williams purchased land from the Narragansetts in present-day Rhode Island, where he established the English settlement of Providence. Over nearly the next five decades, Williams continued to maintain peaceful relations with the Narragansetts and even learned their language.

signaling to the Pequots (and the Pequots' rivals) that the English intended to become a permanent power in the region.

The Pequots' shaky position emphasized how the Narragansett had become the most powerful tribe in southern New England by 1636. The Narragansetts at that point dominated the still-lucrative fur trade with the Dutch. They had also established excellent relations with the English through Roger Williams, who had been expelled from Massachusetts Bay Colony and, with other exiles, created a new colony of English dissidents in Narragansett territory. When English trader John Oldham was found murdered on his ship near Block Island, the Narragansett leaders to whom the Block Islanders gave tribute and allegiance were the obvious suspects. But the Narragansetts were no longer willing to alienate the English colonists. They saw a way to advance their own interests by promising Massachusetts Bay Colony officials to seek revenge against the Pequots for apparently harboring those responsible for Oldham's murder. Massachusetts Bay Colony leaders remained suspicious of the Narragansetts' complicity in the deed, however, and were also interested in undermining the autonomy of the dissident colony as well as parts of Narragansett territory.

WAR COMES TO THE PEQUOTS

In August 1636, Massachusetts dispatched an expedition under John Endecott to obtain revenge for Oldham's death. After finding the Block Island villages deserted, Endecott proceeded to Connecticut to demand satisfaction from the Pequots. Negotiations went nowhere and the English prepared for battle. Their raids on nearby Pequot villages accomplished little but to "raise these wasps about my ears," as Fort Saybrook commander Lion Gardener had feared. The Pequots began raiding English settlements, including Plymouth trading posts, and killing isolated colonists in the area. The Pequots also sought to establish an alliance with the

Narragansetts against the English, arguing that "the English were strangers, and began to overspread their country, and would deprive them thereof in time, if they were suffered to grow and increase; and if the Narragansetts did assist the English to subdue them, that did but make way for their own overthrow; for if they were rooted out, the English would soon take occasion to subjugate them."[2] But in October, through the agency of Williams and the Massachusett sachem Cutshamekin, Massachusetts Bay Colony officials persuaded four Narragansetts—Miantonomo, two sons of Canonicus, and Cutshamekin—to sign a treaty in which they agreed to fully support the colonists in their war against the Pequots. The Narragansetts and Massachusetts were apparently English allies. The Pequots continued to attack English outposts, and in February 1637 surrounded and tried to cut off Fort Saybrook.

As winter turned to spring, Pequot raids intensified; on April 23, they attacked Wethersfield and killed nine colonists. This attack led Connecticut and Massachusetts to mobilize and raise an army, and to seek Plymouth's assistance. Connecticut enlisted the eager assistance offered by the Mohegan sachem Uncas, and Massachusetts tried to cement its unstable alliance with the Narragansetts. Ironically, given postwar antagonisms, Miantonomo was the colonists' greatest supporter in Narragansett councils. In early May, both colonies sent forces to Fort Saybrook, totaling 90 men, joined by 70 Mohegans. Connecticut Colony military commander John Mason decided to avoid a potentially disastrous direct attack on Sassacus's village, and instead took a ship to Narragansett Bay, where the group could ask Miantonomo for warriors and attack the Pequots from the east. The Narragansett sachem was initially reluctant to take a direct role in the campaign, but two days later a band of Narragansetts caught up with the English at an eastern Niantic village and enthusiastically joined the small army.

After a long march, the force attacked and destroyed the Pequot fort on Mystic River on May 26, using surprise, fire, and ruthless slaughter to kill about 600 or 700 inhabitants, mostly women and children, since Sassacus and his main body of warriors had gone to another village, Weinshauks. The English tactics and their massacre of the Pequots horrified their Native American allies, who "much rejoiced at our victories, and greatly admired the manner of *English* mens fight: but cried *mach it, mach it*; that is, it is naught, it is naught, because it is too furious, and slays too many men."[3] Many Narragansetts left, leaving the Puritan–Indian force greatly weakened and vulnerable, particularly when about 300 Pequots came upon their rear as they began retreating toward the Thames River. A brief firefight and the surprise of what had happened at Mystic kept the Pequots at a distance. Word of the staggering Pequot defeat spread quickly, and three days later the Montauk leader Wyandanch went to Fort Saybrook to ensure good relations with the English colonists.

The Pequots at Weinshauks were shocked and horrified by their defeat. They held a meeting to discuss whether to attack the Narragansetts, attack the English, or seek safety to the west. Sassacus "was all for bloud, the rest for flight, alledging these arguments, wee are a people bereaved of courage, our hearts are sadded with the death of so many of our deare friends; wee see upon what advantage the English lye, what sudden & deadly blowes they strike? What advantage they have of their peeces to us which are not able to

---

(opposite page) This map details the primary battles of the Pequot War (1636–37) and the route that Captain John Mason, the leader of Connecticut Colony's forces, took in his pursuit of the Pequots as they fled toward New York. The most tragic event of the war took place on May 26, 1637, at a Pequot village near present-day Mystic, Connecticut, where 600 to 700 residents (mainly women and children) were killed by the English.

reach them at a distance?"[4] They were unable to agree on a single course of action. Some fled to Long Island, Block Island, or sought refuge with the Narragansetts rather than

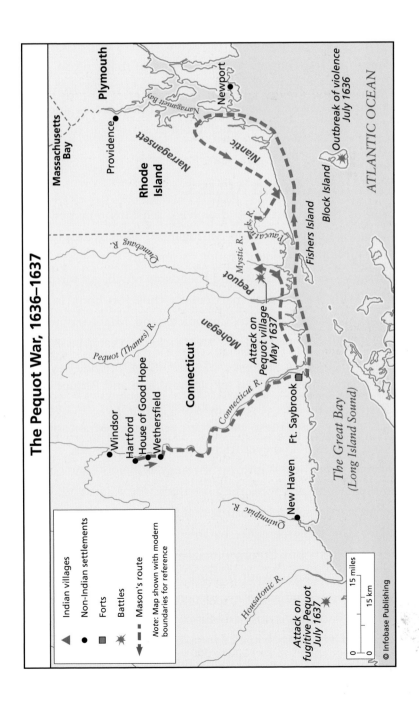

face the English or Mohegans. The largest group, with about 300 men and led by Sassacus, headed west hoping to join the Mohawks (who lived in present-day eastern New York State), but were closely followed by Mohegan bands and soon by a fresh colonial force. On July 14, another major battle at a swamp west of Quinnipiac (now New Haven) resulted in the capture of 180 Pequots and the killing of many more. Sassacus escaped with his brother and other Pequot sachems, and finally reached Mohawk country. But there he and his party were set upon and slaughtered by those who he hoped would provide refuge.

STRAINS AMONG ALLIES

Even as the Pequot tribe dissolved, tensions emerged between the English and their Narragansett allies as they began to compete for Pequot spoils—wampum (currency) and warriors—and the tribute and friendship of villages formerly allied with the Pequots, particularly those on Long Island. Roger Williams met with Canonicus and Miantonomo on August 20, and warned the two sachems that Massachusetts Bay Colony officials were particularly angered. The two Narragansetts denied taking wampum and Pequot captives secretly, listed "many particulars, wherein the English had broken [since these wars] their promises—Miantonomo asked Williams "Did ever friends deal so with friends?"—and warned Governor Winthrop through Williams that Uncas and his Mohegans were the false ones.[5] By August 12, Mohegan warriors were reporting that Mohawks had killed Sassacus. The disagreements between the Narragansetts and Massachusetts Bay Colony officials were seemingly resolved when Miantonomo went to Boston on November 9, 1637. Miantonomo reaffirmed his recognition of Massachusetts's rights to Pequot territory and Block Island, and the colonists agreed to let him seek justice for acts perpetrated against the colonists by Wequash and the Niantic sachem Ninigret.

The Pequot tribe was soon declared extinct, and the Puritan colonies initially insisted on every survivor joining a "friendly" tribe. Uncas exerted considerable effort in gathering as many as possible; some historians believe that he wished to become sachem of a reconstituted Pequot tribe under his "Mohegan" banner. Mohegan tradition indicates that these adoptees continued for generations to retain a separate, lower status within the tribe. Others joined the Niantics or Narragansetts, or took to canoes to seek refuge on Block Island or Long Island. Connecticut tried to keep Pequot territory clear for their colonists, and, after receiving word in 1639 that some Pequots were attempting to resettle there, sent a large force under John Mason and Uncas to evict what turned out to be Niantics and Narragansetts. This incident and other efforts by the English to deny hunting rights to the Narragansetts in Pequot territory certainly increased that tribe's growing resentment toward the English.

The Pequot tribe did not remain extinct for very long. Within five years, the United Colonies of New England (Massachusetts Bay, Plymouth, Connecticut, and New Haven) found it useful to allow the reconstitution of two Pequot groups under the leadership of Wequash (soon succeeded by Caushawashott, better known as Harmon Garrett) and Robin Cassasinamon, the former having assisted the English during the conflict, and the latter having spent eight years as a servant in the Winthrop household. Both Pequot groups were created in part to counter the potential threat of an overly ambitious Uncas, and to provide reliable protection for the infant English settlements in Pequot territory. The two bands would, during the following few decades, become the Stonington (or Lantern Hill) and Nameag (or Mashantucket) Pequot communities. In 1638, though, Roger Williams reported five separate surviving Pequot groups along the Thames River, in addition to those living with Uncas or Ninigret, on Long Island, and elsewhere.

Uncas and his Mohegans continued to pressure the Pequot remnants, occasionally assaulting their villages and attacking individuals. When the Pequots and their English neighbors formally complained to United Colony officials, the commissioners rebuked Uncas and arranged a treaty that provided autonomy and reservations for Wequash and Cassasinamon in exchange for tribute paid to Uncas. But Uncas still occasionally harassed the Pequots. In September 1654, the commissioners declared the Pequot remnants under their protection, which seems to have been the final shift in the status of the Pequot remnants from semisovereign communities to groups that were clearly tributaries of the United Colonies. One month later, confederation delegates collected Pequots who had been living under Ninigret's rule and made them officially subjects of the confederation, living in Connecticut. In September 1655, the commissioners officially "appointed" Wequash and Cassasinamon heads of their communities and issued rules for the latter that included an end to powwows and "blaspheming"—that is, traditional Native American holidays and ceremonies. Three years later, the Pequots got the United Colonies to pressure Wyandanch and the Montauks to give them access to the wampum shell beds on Long Island.

The war eliminated the Pequot tribe as a power and thus, as the victors hoped, opened new opportunities in the region. The Mohegans displaced the Pequots as the leading Native American group along the Thames River, and Uncas used his loyalty to the English as a lever to increase his power throughout Connecticut and beyond. Ninigret, who had remained neutral in the war but had kinship relations with the Pequots and Narragansetts, gained new influence among the Narragansetts and prominence with the English. The English were clearly the greatest beneficiaries, having destroyed a major barrier to their expansion into Connecticut and becoming the greatest power in southern New England. But the

The Pequot War devastated the Pequots and forced many to take refuge with the Narragansetts or flee to Long Island or Block Island. This illustration depicts the attack by Connecticut Colony forces on the Pequots' village on Mystic River in May 1637.

dynamics of the war and its aftermath also sowed the seeds of future conflicts. The English taxed each surviving Pequot, and the sachem of the tribe or village where the survivors lived became responsible for paying the correct amount of tribute. This annual tribute became a major issue for the Indian leaders. The war generally reshaped relationships between different Native American communities, scrambling tribal alliances and boundaries along both sides of Long Island Sound and providing a new opening to English settlements on eastern Long Island.

The most important issue, and one that would play a role in King Philip's War, was the conflict between Uncas and Miantonomo. This conflict worsened as the Pequot War ground to an end. Both sought to adopt as many Pequot captives as possible in order to build up strength, and both tried to persuade his English allies that the other was not trustworthy. Other tribes and villages found themselves forced into involvement. Massasoit traveled to Boston on April 21, 1638, to meet with Governor Winthrop, giving beaver skins and getting reassurance of peace. The Niantics took advantage of the chaos to try and force the Montauks on Long Island into tributary status, angering Connecticut leaders who threatened Ninigret with war unless he made amends—which he did. In September 1638, Connecticut demanded that both Miantonomo and Uncas come to Hartford to settle their problems. The resulting treaty between the English and Narragansetts and Mohegans declared an end to that conflict and required the tribes' leaders to submit all future complaints to "the English" before taking action; gave both tribes an equal number of the remaining Pequots and required that a tax be paid to "the English" for each Pequot they held; claimed Pequot territory for the English; and declared the Pequot tribe extinct.

Puritan Power Expands, 1640–1660

Despite the treaty of Hartford, tensions quickly developed between the Narragansetts and the Puritan leaders who disliked the tribe's independence and close alliances with dissidents like Roger Williams. The resulting conflicts meshed with colonial expansion in the region to build English power and form the relationships that would help shape King Philip's War. By the summer of 1640, the English believed that Miantonomo was forging a hostile alliance with the feared Mohawks. Massachusetts Bay Colony sent a delegation to visit Miantonomo, and although Miantonomo and his sachems agreed to all of their demands, a second meeting at Boston turned sour when the English violated protocol.

The Narragansetts were increasingly angered at colonists' support for Uncas, demands for large amounts of tribute, and spreading settlements. In mid-1642, Miantonomo visited the Montauks on Long Island and urged them to unite against the English, "for so are we all Indians as the English are, and say brother to one another; so must we be one as they are, otherwise we shall be gone shortly, for you know our fathers had plenty of deer and skins, our plains were full of deer, as also our woods, and of turkies, and our coves full of fish and fowl. But these English having gotten our land, they with scythes cut down the grass, and with axes fell the trees; their cows and horses eat the grass, and their hogs spoil our clam banks, and we shall all be starved."[6]

English fears of an uprising crested in August 1642, when Connecticut warned Massachusetts of a pan-tribal conspiracy and urged a preemptive strike against the Narragansetts. But Massachusetts Bay Colony leaders suspected that Uncas started the rumors to manipulate the English, and so met with Miantonomo who "offered to meet Onkus" before the colonists in order to "prove to his face his treachery against the English."[7] They told their Connecticut counterparts to back off from war.

Massachusetts also continued its efforts to isolate and weaken the dangerous Narragansetts. On April 22, 1642, the colony gained the allegiance of two sachems in northeastern Rhode Island, chopping away at the Narragansett confederacy and allowing officials in Boston to arrest a small settlement of English radicals in the area. Roger Williams rushed to England to gain the protection of a charter for the dissident colony and its Narragansett allies. In response, Massachusetts, Connecticut, New Haven, and Plymouth joined in mid-1643 in a "firm and perpetual League of Friendship and Amity for offense and defense." (Rhode Island was not invited to join the United Colonies.)

In July 1643, the long-simmering conflict between the Mohegans and Narragansetts flared into open war. Uncas complained to Connecticut that he had been attacked by a Wongunk war party along the Connecticut River, and obtained permission to take revenge. Miantonomo, committed to protecting the Wongunks, obtained permission from Massachusetts to strike at Uncas. But the Mohegans defeated the Narragansett war party and captured Miantonomo. Uncas

Miantonomo, the Narragansett sachem, and Uncas, the Mohegan sachem, emerged as the two strongest leaders in the wake of the defeat of the Pequots. In July 1643, Uncas captured Miantonomo and was given permission to execute the Narragansett sachem, which is depicted in this woodcut.

took Miantonomo to Boston, probably because he was confident that the English wanted the sachem dead. The very first decision United Colony officials made was to authorize the execution of Miantonomo by Uncas's warriors. The English promised Uncas that they would send soldiers if necessary to protect him and his tribe from Narragansett revenge.

MIANTONOMO AND UNCAS

In the wake of the Pequot War, Puritan leaders believed that the powerful Narragansett sachem Miantonomo was attempting to form an alliance with the Mohawks. For their part, the Narragansetts were increasingly angered at the colonists' support for the upstart and arrogant Mohegan sachem Uncas. In mid-1643, all of the New England colonies but Rhode Island joined in a committee to coordinate policies and actions with the Indians. Their first challenge came in July, when the ongoing conflict between the Mohegans and Narragansetts resulted in war. A war party led by Miantonomo was defeated by the Mohegans, who captured the Narragansett sachem. Uncas took him to Boston, where the very first decision by the United Colonies was to authorize his execution.

September 7, 1643

[F]rom tyme to tyme we have taken notice of the violation of that league betweene the Massachusets and [the Narragansetts], (notwithstanding the manefestations of love and integryty towards them by the English) which they have discovered as by other wayes, so lately by their concurrance with Myantenomo their Sachim in his mischeevous plotts . . . And whereas Uncus was advised to take away the life of Myantenomo whose lawfull Captive he was, They may well understand that this is without violation of any Covenant betweene them and us for Uncus being in confedation with us, and one that hath dilligently observed his Covenants before mentioned for ought we know, and requireing advice from

After Miantonomo's death, the Narragansetts continued to press their case against Uncas. In 1643 and 1644, the new Narragansett sachem Canonicus sought the approval of the United Colonies to attack Uncas. The commissioners refused and threatened war, in part because they suspected the Narragansetts were plotting with the Mohawks. The Narragansetts

us upon serious consideration of the premisss, viz. his treacherous and murtherous Disposition against Uncus etc. and how great A Disturber hee hath beene of the Comon peace of the whole Countrey . . .

That as soone as the Comissioners for Coneetacutt and New Haven shall returne into those parts that then Uncas be sent for to Hartford with some considerable number of his best and trustyest men, and that then he being made acquainted with the advice of the Comissioners Myantenomo be delivered unto him that so execution may be donn according to justice and prudence Uncus carrying him into the next part of his owne goverment and there put him to death Provided that some discreet and faythfull persons of the English accompany them and see the execution for our more full satisfaction, and that the English meddle not with the head or body at all . . .

Hartford [shall] furnish Uncus with a competent strengh of English to defend him against any present fury or assault of the Nanohiggunsets or any other . . . Plymouth [shall] labour by all due meanes to restore Woosamequin [Massasoit] to his full liberties in respect of any encroachments by the Nanohiggansets or any other Natives that so the proprieties of the Indians may be preserved to themselves, and that no one Sagomore encroach upon the rest as of late: And that Woosamequin be reduced to these former termes and agreements betweene Plymouth and him.[*]

[signed, Commissioners of the United Colonies]

---

[*] Nathaniel B. Shurtleff, ed., *Records of the Colony of New Plymouth, in New England,* vol. 9 (Boston: W. White, 1855–61), 14–15.

responded by treating the Massachusetts Bay Colony's delegation rudely, declaring war on the Mohegans (raiding that tribe and killing 11), and in April 1644 making a formal *"voluntary and free submission"* to King Charles II in an effort to gain England's protection against the United Colonies. Canonicus, Pessicus, and their counselors noted their "jealousy and suspicion of some of His Majesty's pretended subjects"—that is, the Puritans of Massachusett Bay Colony—and declared that they could not *"yield over ourselves unto any that are subjects themselves in any case*; having ourselves been the chief sachems, or princes successfully, and of the country, time out of mind."[8]

In response, the United Colonies called Canonicus to Boston, but the Narragansett sachem instead sent a message that "wee have subjected ourselves, our lands, and our possessions" to King Charles, so that if the colony had any problems with the tribe they should submit the issue to the king to decide between the two equally sovereign governments.[9] This is hardly what the Puritans wanted to hear, and not surprisingly the United Colonies announced that they would assist the Mohegans if they were attacked by the Narragansetts. In February 1645, Canonicus sent messengers to Boston to demand tribute from Uncas. When he received nothing, a large Narragansett force attacked the Mohegans. The battle lasted all day and resulted in heavy losses for both tribes, but forced the Narragansetts to retreat. In July, the United Colonies summoned the hostile parties to a conference in Boston, but also prepared to attack the Narragansetts and their allies the Niantics. The English called off the attack after the Narragansetts' leaders suddenly appeared, but the commissioners refused to hear complaints against Uncas. The commissioners also demanded hostages, 2,000 fathoms of wampum (one fathom was equivalent to a six-foot length of wampum, which included about 360 beads), reparations for the Mohegans, and the surrender of all rights to Pequot territory. Canonicus and the others signed under duress, realizing that the alternative was a disastrous war.

The Boston conference and treaty settled nothing. In June 1646, United Colony commissioners accused the Narragansetts and Niantics of breaking the treaty, and three months later formally notified both tribes that they had not met the treaty terms and were suspected of plotting with the Mohawks. A year later, the United Colonies again sent word to both tribes that they had violated their treaty obligations and were suspected of plotting an attack. The English demanded a meeting. Canonicus found a polite way of refusing to appear but sent delegates; Ninigret went to the conference and agreed to stay there while messengers went to the two tribes to obtain the wampum owed to the United Colonies. They returned two weeks later with 200 fathoms of wampum, half from each tribe. Ninigret promised to gather more if he could return home. The commissioners agreed, but threatened war if a thousand fathoms more did not arrive within 20 days. As before, that deadline passed without retribution, because the English and Indians both wished to avoid war.

THE COLD WAR EXPANDS

In 1646, the conflict between Uncas and the Narragansetts again involved Indians along the Connecticut River and rumors of Mohawk involvement. The commissioners discovered a plot by Sequasson, the Wongunk sachem, to assassinate several Connecticut magistrates in retaliation for their support of the judicial murder of Miantonomo. Sequasson fled to a Pocumtuck village, but Uncas attacked the village and captured the Wongunk sachem. Sequasson was put on trial but was (amazingly) acquitted, and apparently ended his enmity against the English. Uncas continued to warn that the Pocumtucks and Wongunks were up to no good, but few colonists believed the Mohegan, particularly after other Indian groups such as the Nipmucs lodged complaints against

Although he did not participate in the Pequot War, Niantic sachem Ninigret benefited greatly from the defeat of the Pequots. Ninigret aligned himself with the Narragansetts and, along with his rival Uncas, became one of the more influential sachems of southern New England.

his warriors. Still, the English continued to be very sensitive to stories of broad conspiracies to attack the colonies. That same summer, for example, a Mohawk band visited the Pocumtucks. The Narragansett sachems sent a gift of wampum that seems to have been a traditional courtesy or possibly a tribute, leading to a rumor that the tribes were plotting to war against the Mohegans and the English. The Narragansett sachems were luckily able to persuade the English that the wampum was an annual gift to the Mohawks.

The fears of the commissioners that Ninigret and the Narragansetts were becoming a danger were magnified by the way in which the tribes and Rhode Island's disruptive dissidents supported each other. On May 28, 1650, Rhode Island and the Narragansetts signed a treaty. Three months later the United Colonies dispatched a delegation to demand the outstanding 308 fathoms of wampum from the Narragansetts, and authorized Massachusetts to begin preparations for war. The Narragansett sachems again reached an agreement that prevented war, despite being abused by the head of the Massachusetts delegation. In 1656, the Narragansett–Mohegan conflict flared again as Mixanno (Canonicus's eldest son) charged Uncas with "abusively naming and Jeering his dead Ancestors" and challenged the sachem to battle.[10] A new war was avoided as the English promised to look into the charges, told the Narragansetts not to attack Uncas, and rebuked the Mohegan for provoking the Narragansetts.

But their conflict again spilled over in the Connecticut River Valley in May, after a young man killed a relative of Sequasson and fled to a Pocumtuck village. Sequasson asked his former enemy Uncas to help him obtain justice, and despite an effort by Connecticut to mediate, Sequasson insisted on blood vengeance rather than compensation. For the next few years the Pocumtucks, joined by Tunxis and Narragansett warriors, continued to attack the Mohegans, occasionally frightening colonial settlers in the area. In September 1658, the United Colonies told the tribes to keep their conflict away from English settlements, and demanded a meeting. A year later, the Pocumtucks told the English that they had not harmed the colonists or their cattle, and could not negotiate a treaty nor stop hostilities against the Mohegans without the approval of their allies. Tensions escalated when Pocumtuck warriors attacked an English trading outpost on Mohegan territory because, they told the United Colonies, the trader had provided Uncas with weapons and was sheltering 20 Mohegans.

The result was the infamous Atherton Deed of 1660, which added to the long list of Narragansett grievances. The United Colonies decided the Narragansetts were the real culprits in the Pocumtuck conflict, and fined them the huge sum of 595 fathoms of wampum, with the threat of war if they refused to pay. On September 29, 1660, three Narragansett sachems agreed to pay the fine within four months; if they did not, they would lose their remaining lands, about 400 square miles (more than 1,000 square kilometers). Two years earlier, a group of prominent Puritans from several colonies had established the Narragansett Proprietors, better known as the Atherton Company, to profit from Narragansett lands and undercut Rhode Island and Narragansett authority. The proprietors agreed to pay the Narragansetts' fine in exchange for a mortgage on their tribal lands, which extended the time for the loan to six months. But the tribe was still unable to pay, and the proprietors claimed their prize in 1662. As a result, the region became mired in legal and jurisdictional controversies that endangered the Narragansetts and Rhode Island, and which were not resolved by a royal commission in 1664 that rejected the Atherton Deed as fraudulent. In the meantime, the Pocumtucks had become involved in a costly war with the Mohawks, and by 1665 had been driven from several of their villages. Puritan settlers quickly built their own villages on those sites and rejected efforts by the Pocumtucks to return, leading to devastating attacks by the tribe during King Philip's War.

ENGLISH COLONIAL EXPANSION

In the middle of the sevententh century, colonists established many new settlements in the interior of New England, generating more conflicts largely because of differences between English and Native American concepts of ownership. Indians generally signed deeds expecting to share the resources on the land, not to transfer the area to full and absolute English ownership. Clashes also resulted from the trespass of English cattle and pigs into Indian cornfields and, as colonial settlements grew, neighboring Native Americans increasingly did not have enough land to meet their own needs. Colonial leaders began to assume that they could readily obtain Indian land. The uncertain or contested nature of land ownership could also lead to intersecting or clashing rights claimed by different sachems. Competition between the colonies, communities, and individuals could also cause conflicts as Indian leaders accused each other of fraud for selling land they did not own—sometimes, one suspects, at the behest of a competing colony. As good land became scarcer by the mid-1600s, colonists seeking advantages sometimes attempted to use Indian titles to secure their claims against others. Indian leaders also sought to gain political or economic advantages by manipulating the ambitions, jealousies, and quarrels of the colonists.

These dealings over land between the Pequot and King Philip's wars were not just about who held, worked, and benefited from the land. Issues of political power and sovereignty were deeply embedded in land transactions, as well as the treaties. The colonists clearly believed that land deeds or treaties recognizing colonial authority conveyed sovereignty as well as ultimate tenure to them. But the sachems who put their marks to such agreements—assuming that they accurately understood the words on the paper—seem to have perceived their resulting relationship with the colony as either allies or, at worst, that their tribes would become tributaries of the English but would not surrender their sovereignty or their land. Still, by 1650, the English colonists had, with considerable success, greatly expanded their diplomatic and military influence. Massachusetts and Connecticut were clearly the dominant powers in the region, and in tandem with New Haven and Plymouth held even more potential through the United Colonies.

But more than diplomacy and military force influenced peoples and events in the region. Trade, law, and religion all played major roles in shaping relationships between Native Americans and newcomers. Trading had always served multiple purposes: meeting the economic needs or desires of those involved in the trade, serving peace or generating new conflicts, and acting as avenues for daily contact and cultural diffusion. As a result, trading posts played a major role in diplomacy and war in the region. Law served as a tool of colonial domination. In 1621, Plymouth began by making any crime between an Indian and a colonist subject to their law, and throughout the rest of the century, the English built up their expectations and their system of legal domination within their area of influence.

Puritan missionaries represented another important element of colonial expansion and influence in the region. John Eliot's story is particularly well known. He learned the native language from a Pequot War captive. He then approached the Massachusett sachem Cutshamekin but was spurned. Later, in 1647, he traveled to Nonantum, a Massachusett village near Nipmuc territory. One of its leading men, Waban, embraced Eliot and his message, and the Puritan minister drew a curious crowd that grew at each subsequent visit. In 1651, Waban and Eliot founded the "praying town" of Natick, which drew so many Indians that Cutshamekin felt compelled to publicly embrace Eliot's Christianity in order to reassert his tribal authority. The multifaceted success of these missionary efforts encouraged Eliot to seek converts in other villages. By the 1670s, five "praying towns" formed an arch about 30 miles from Boston, including Pennacook and Nipmuc villages, and edging into Wampanoag territory. In 1674, Eliot and others visited the Pennacooks, and then traveled deep into Nipmuc territory to install Christian Indian teachers and preachers in various villages. This missionary enterprise would become another important factor in King Philip's War.

Despite the expansion and growing power of English settlements, their authority was certainly not supreme. In the 1660s, the Narragansett (like other tribes) continued to insist on their autonomy, and in November 1663, gained formal recognition of their sovereignty from the newly restored English king Charles II. The Narragansetts' primary concern, as emphasized in their reply of thanks for the king's "gracious protection," was to regain their lands from the Atherton mortgage and similar deeds. The occasional threat of Mohawks in the region also continued to keep the colonists on their toes. Even Uncas and his Mohegans were not completely under English domination, as he demonstrated in 1674, when his emissaries demanded that Eliot stay out of Mohegan territory. The Wampanoags similarly maneuvered to maintain their autonomy. Metacom's efforts to retain his power against Plymouth's aggression would lead to King Philip's War and ultimately attract the support of the Nipmuc, Narragansett, Pocumtuck, and other tribes.

War Clouds Build, 1660–1675

THE CONFLICT BETWEEN THE WAMPANOAGS AND Plymouth Colony that exploded into King Philip's War followed the death of Massasoit around 1660. At that time, his eldest son, Wamsutta, informed Plymouth that he was now sachem and, in accordance with Native American custom, asked for a new name as a token of the change and a reaffirmation of the Wampanoags' alliance with the colony. The English, thinking of ancient Greek history, gave Wamsutta the name of Alexander, and (for some reason) gave his younger brother Metacom the name of Alexander's father, Philip. Historians do not know which name Metacom preferred, nor what other Indians called him.

This auspicious beginning did not last, in part because of events in England, and in part because of developments within the region. In 1660, 11 years after Parliament had executed King Charles I during the English Civil War, a new Parliament more concerned about disorder invited Charles II to return from exile in France and restore the monarchy. This restoration endangered Plymouth Colony because it had never

Wamsutta, the eldest son of Massasoit, became sachem of the Wampanoags after Massasoit's death in 1660. However, after selling land to Rhode Island colonists in 1662, he was reprimanded by Plymouth officials and was asked to meet with them. On his way to the meeting, he mysteriously became ill and died during the trip back.

obtained a charter, and some of its leaders had supported the rebels against Charles I. The colony had depended on its diplomatic relations with the Wampanoags for its legal existence and its claimed borders as far as Narragansett Bay, and was thus alarmed at the potential threat of the new king's hostility. The tribe's territory formed a border zone between Plymouth, Rhode Island, and Massachusetts, each of which wanted the area. Thus, when Wamsutta sold some land to Rhode Island colonists in July 1662, Plymouth leaders became quite nervous. They asked the sachem not to deal with anyone but them, but eight days later he sold more land to Rhode Island. Josiah Winslow, the son of the Plymouth governor and the commander of the colony's militia, took an armed party to force Wamsutta to come to Plymouth in order to intimidate the sachem. They found Wamsutta at a hunting station; he agreed to go with them, but once under way became very sick. Alarmed, Winslow released the sachem, who died while on the way home.

METACOM IN CHARGE AND BESIEGED

Plymouth immediately summoned Wamsutta's brother and successor to answer charges of conspiring against the English. No doubt thinking of his brother's fate, Metacom came on his own and quickly agreed to a treaty that continued the existing agreements but also added a clause that he would never sell land without Plymouth's permission. The new sachem was probably deceived about the wording of the 1662 treaty, because six months later he dictated a letter to the colony that referred to the ban as lasting only seven years. About that time, Connecticut obtained a new royal charter that gave it New Haven. More ominously, a year later, Rhode Island obtained a charter that placed some of the territory claimed by Plymouth, including Metacom's home village of Sowams on the Mount Hope Peninsula, within its boundaries. Plymouth still did not have a charter or any right under English law to its territory. They therefore must have been alarmed at the arrival in 1664 of commissioners sent by Charles II to inspect and ensure the loyalty of his colonies—particularly after Metacom obtained the commissioners' support for his autonomy and rights to land. The Narragansetts took similar action and won the Crown's official support.

During the next decade, Metacom maneuvered to maintain his authority and his people's welfare as the English population and power grew. His tribal confederacy splintered under the persistent influence of colonial authorities and missionaries. In part to retain influence in these treacherous currents, Metacom sold tracts of land to various colonists and English investors. Conflicts over the uncertain borders that followed, however, were rarely settled to his satisfaction, because colonial courts seemed biased. The Indians were also angered by the attitudes and policies of Plymouth authorities, who in many little decisions and actions showed that they felt they had the right to obtain Wampanoag territory and resources at will. Additional strife developed as English livestock wandered onto Indian fields and ate their corn. Native Americans responded by confiscating or killing the animals. In response to these problems, some Indians, including Metacom, began raising pigs, creating new sources of competition for resources. In the 1660s, Plymouth expanded existing towns and created new ones, making the Wampanoags feel as if they were being forcibly cornered on the Mount Hope Peninsula (in present-day Rhode Island).

Tensions noticeably increased in 1667 as Plymouth established the town of Swansea, which was within both Metacom's territory and Rhode Island's jurisdiction under its 1663 charter. Plymouth was understandably worried about the response of the Wampanoag sachem. That summer the colony's leaders quickly reacted to word from one of Metacom's warriors that the sachem was conspiring with either the Dutch or the French. When the colony sent delegates to confront Metacom, he denied the story, blamed Ninigret (whom the Wampanoags had long disliked) for hiring the man to accuse him, and offered to surrender his firearms to the English as proof of his fidelity. Plymouth accepted this offer, and told the sachem to appear at the colonial assembly's next meeting. Metacom appeared and again swore "love and faithfulness to the English, and that [the rumor] was a meer plot of Ninnegrett." Plymouth officials went to question Ninigret, who denied the accusation. Without any other evidence, the colony decided to trust Metacom for the moment and to return his weapons, but charged him £40 for the investigation.

In the meantime, Swansea settlers and other Plymouth colonists continued to seek land. Metacom and his warriors, angered by this challenge to tribal authority and territory, and the apparent violation of the 1662 treaty, paraded through Swansea with their weapons threateningly displayed. Plymouth reacted by demanding that Metacom come to the town of Taunton in April 1671. One month before the scheduled conference, the colony's magistrates called on the sachem to answer a colonist's complaint against one of his people. Not only did Metacom refuse, but his warriors threatened the colony's delegate and appeared to be preparing for war. At the April conference, surrounded by the hostile English, Metacom signed a treaty that, by acknowledging his violation of past agreements with Plymouth, accepted the colony's view that he had been a subject rather than a sovereign; he also agreed to surrender his men's muskets. Everyone in the region seemed to recognize, however, that this "treaty" only sharpened the conflict, and stories circulated that Metacom's warriors still had many firearms. Plymouth leaders demonstrated their anxiety by quickly obtaining agreements of loyalty from the sachems of villages along outer Cape Cod, the lower Cape, and the west side of the colony, as well as their promises to inform the colony of any threat.

Five months later, bolstered by the treaties obtained during the summer and alarmed by rumors of warriors gathering at Mount Hope, Plymouth sent James Brown and John Walker to call Metacom to a conference to answer charges that he was violating the agreement he made in April. They found the sachem and his people in a dance, most of them drunk; when Brown attempted to speak with Metacom, the sachem knocked his hat off, probably claiming the same deference due any English sovereign or magistrate. The next day Brown returned, but Metacom informed Plymouth's delegate that he had already been invited by John Eliot and the Christian Indians to go to Boston and have Massachusetts mediate his conflict with Plymouth. The following Tuesday, Metacom met with Massachusetts Bay Colony leaders to complain about Plymouth's infringements on his sovereignty. Massachusetts asked Plymouth to avoid war and to meet with Metacom at the end of September. But the sachem's reprieve did not last.

On September 29, 1671, authorities from Massachusetts, Connecticut, and New Haven confronted Metacom and, after hearing Plymouth's charges, compelled him to sign a new treaty. It began with his promise that he, his council, and his "subjects"—a very broad term that could be interpreted to mean all Indians in Plymouth Colony—"doe acknowledge ourselves subjects to his ma[jes]tie. the Kinge of England, etc., and the government of New Plymouth, and to theire lawes." He promised to pay the Plymouth government £100 "in such thinges as I have," which by 1671 meant land. He also promised that he would submit any conflict between his people and any English colonists to the governor of New Plymouth, "not to make warr with any but with the Governors approbation," and "not to dispose of any of the lands that I have att present, but by the approbation of the government of New Plymouth." The treaty was designed to force the Wampanoags into subjection to Plymouth and prevent them from becoming allies of Rhode Island.[11]

SASSAMON MURDERED, METACOM TRIED

As Plymouth pushed harder on Wampanoag sovereignty and territory, Massachusetts extended its authority west, south, and north with settlements and missionaries. In addition to establishing Pennacook, Massachusett, and Nipmuc praying towns, Eliot trained Christian Indians to become missionaries to expand the influence of the English religion and culture. One of the most prominent was John Sassamon. His parents were among the earliest Native American converts to Christianity before they died. Left an orphan, Sassamon was raised in an English household. In 1637, he served the colonists as an interpreter and warrior during the Pequot campaign. He was fluent in spoken and written English, and while living in Dorchester after the war, he became close to Eliot, who lived in nearby Roxbury. Sassamon embraced Christianity, became Natick's first schoolmaster, and was educated at Harvard College. In 1662, he entered Wamsutta's service and then remained as Metacom's scribe and translator, playing a major role in the sachem's negotiations with Plymouth. But Metacom became angered at Sassamon's efforts to convert him and his people to Christianity, which challenged Metacom's authority, and also suspected that Sassamon was taking advantage of his illiteracy (secretly writing the sachem's will in order to gain most of his territory) and generally scheming with the colonists. In 1671, the sachem dismissed Sassamon, who went to live in a cabin on the shore of Assawompsett Pond in the area between Plymouth and the Wampanoags. Here, he ministered to the Christian Indian community at Namasket.

On a cold late January morning in 1675, Sassamon made the 15-mile journey to Plymouth. There he sought and obtained a meeting with Governor Josiah Winslow, warning that Metacom was creating alliances with other sachems in order to destroy the English. This was not a complete surprise. Stories of armed Wampanoag warriors gathering at Mount Hope and the sachem's efforts to gain the support of other tribes had been common currency for years. Sassamon also told Winslow that he feared Metacom would kill him if his visit became known. The governor dismissed the warning because, he later noted, Indians were rarely believable. But the impact of Sassamon's message grew when he disappeared less than a week later. In February, his body was found under the ice on the pond near his house. While he was quickly buried, Englishmen and Native Americans alike began to discuss the case and many believed that Sassamon had been murdered.

At the end of the month, Metacom voluntarily appeared before Plymouth authorities to answer to charges

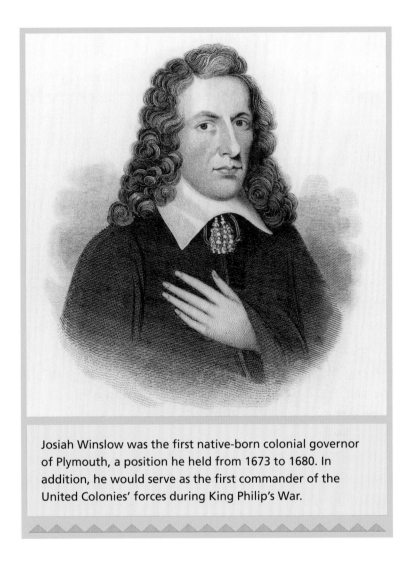

Josiah Winslow was the first native-born colonial governor of Plymouth, a position he held from 1673 to 1680. In addition, he would serve as the first commander of the United Colonies' forces during King Philip's War.

of conspiracy. While the council was not convinced of the sachem's innocence, they lacked proof and sent him home. On March 1, the larger General Court questioned many Indians without finding additional evidence. A few days later, a Christian Indian, Patuckson, appeared and swore that he had seen three of Metacom's counselors (Mattashunannamo, Tobias, and Tobias's son Wampapaquan) kill Sassamon on January 29. On June 1, the three were indicted for murder. The trial took place before an unusual jury of 12 Englishmen and six Indians, and featured both modern and medieval evidence: a coroner's inquest, eyewitness testimony (by Christian Indians), and the fresh bleeding of Sassamon's corpse (exhumed by Plymouth officials for the case) when approached by Tobias. Metacom's counselors denied the charge, and the sachem himself told the colony that if he wanted Sassamon dead it would have been his right by custom and that he did not need to stage an elaborate scenario. But the jury found the three guilty, and they were all hanged on June 8—but not before one, in an effort to save his life, confessed to following Metacom's orders. This was the first English trial of Indian-on-Indian murder, and (in addition to issues of politics and revenge) represented a blatant challenge by Plymouth to Metacom's authority and a declaration that the colony would enforce the power over the Wampanoags that it had claimed four years before.

The Wampanoag sachem was already gathering his warriors and seeking alliances with other tribes against the English. The colonists, anticipating this move, began dispatching delegations to other Native American communities to seek allies or at least neutrality. The often-personal nature of politics and frontier relationships, and the connection between those relationships and state policies, is highlighted by these hurried conferences. Benjamin Church, who had built his home at Sakonnet and in the process developed close relations with the nearby band of Wampanoags known as the Sakonnets, met with their "squaw sachem" Awashonks on June 7 to ask her about the rumors Metacom was "plotting a bloody design." She introduced Church to six "Mount-hope Men" (Wampanoag warriors and ambassadors from Metacom) who had carried the message that the colonists were gathering an army to invade Wampanoag territory. The men had threatened that if she did not join Metacom's alliance, the sachem would send his warriors to kill cattle and burn houses in colonial settlements near her village, "which would provide the English to fall upon her."[12]

After further conversation, she asked Church to negotiate on her behalf with Plymouth, and sent two of her men with him to make sure he was not harmed. Five days later, Roger Williams met with the Narragansett sachem Pessicus (who, in 1647, had changed his name to Canonicus in honor of his deceased uncle) to find out whether Uncas was trying to create an alliance with that tribe. It is likely that the English were concerned that the Mohegans and Narragansetts might join Metacom.

But such negotiations seemed doomed. The trial and hanging of Metacom's counselors flaunted Plymouth's authority over the Wampanoags, and the English were also quite arrogant about their trespass on Native American lands and livelihoods. On June 11, just three days after the execution, John Brown wrote a panicky note from Swansea telling Governor Winslow that the Wampanoags were brandishing their weapons on the outskirts of the town and had taken various measures that promised war within a few days. About five days later, John Easton of Rhode Island led his small band to a ford near Metacom's village to seek a way to prevent the looming hostilities. Unfortunately, while his meeting with the Wampanoag sachem was fairly amiable, his efforts to set up a means to mediate the conflict were unsuccessful. On June 19, Governor Winslow sent a message to Metacom asking the Wampanoags to surrender their arms and meet with the colony. In reply, the sachem denied any hostile intentions but warned that any delegates bearing "harsh threats" would face "great dangers." The governor then contacted his counterpart in Massachusetts, John Leverett, warning of the likely war and asking him to ensure the loyalty of the Nipmuc and Narragansett tribes. Leverett also decided to send delegates led by Captain Thomas Savage to mediate with Metacom, but on their way to Swansea they found the decapitated bodies of two Swansea men in the middle of the road, killed by Wampanoags.

War Begins,
June and July 1675

BY THE SUMMER OF 1675, SWANSEA CONTAINED THREE villages within the larger town boundaries: one around the Miles garrison (a large house with doors and windows reinforced, stocked with food and water, which could serve as a makeshift fort), one around the Bourne garrison, and one along the Kickamuit River, closest to Mount Hope. On Sunday, June 20, eight Wampanoags traveled to the Kickamuit settlement to have their hatchets sharpened. When the blacksmith refused to work on the Sabbath, the Wampanoags became angry and entered another house and took food. The terrified village residents, expecting an attack from Metacom, immediately fled to the Bourne garrison, and Plymouth's governor ordered nearby Bridgewater and Taunton to raise a militia of 200 men.

The next day, some of the militia began arriving. At this point, Wampanoag men began shooting at the garrison sentries and looted and burned more English houses. On June 23, John Salisbury, stationed in the Bourne garrison, shot at several warriors looting an abandoned English home, hitting one. Some Wampanoags approached the garrison and asked if the Englishman had shot the Wampanoag man; Salisbury replied with bravado that "it was no matter." The following day, warriors killed six men, including Salisbury, who had tried to gather food from an abandoned home a quarter-mile away. Later that day, a band surprised a group returning from church, killing one man and wounding others. That night, at the Miles garrison, a sentry was shot and killed by warriors. The English sent for a surgeon in the nearby town of Rehoboth, but the two messengers were killed on the road. Their bodies were found by the Massachusetts delegation the following morning.

The Wampanoags probably killed the men because their wounded warrior had died. Before, the angry warriors had been satisfied with threats and destroying English property. Such violence was symbolic, meant to express and vent a community's rage. For Native Americans in the region, the English houses, cattle, and fences were highly charged symbols of the colonial political, economic, and ecological intrusions that had transformed the area in just a few decades. But Native American culture required revenge or retribution for bloodshed. Even worse, the English had dismissed the matter instead of seeking a settlement. Metacom himself was reportedly not present and probably did not order the initial killings, since he was apparently not yet ready to go to war and seemed interested in Easton's offer of mediation.

On June 26, even before hearing about the deaths, Massachusetts governor John Leverett and his council mustered two militia companies and sent them south to Swansea. They put together a third that evening, perhaps after the colony's delegation returned. The third included 110 men under the command of Captain Samuel Moseley, a tough Jamaican privateer who would be popular with his men but often abused neutral or friendly Indians. Massachusetts colonial forces reached Swansea on June 28. Their unit had more than 350 mounted and foot soldiers, including a number of Indian

During King Philip's War, Captain Benjamin Church served as the primary aid to Governor Winslow and was part of the first military unit in America to invade Indian territory. In 1716, Church's son Thomas published *Entertaining Passages Relating to Philip's War*, which was largely adapted from his father's notes of the war.

allies. Despite their numbers, they remained pinned inside the garrisons. After a second sentry at the Miles garrison was hit, some cavalrymen commanded by Thomas Prentice decided (along with Benjamin Church) to seek out and attack the snipers in the woods across the bridge from the garrison house. But some warriors were waiting, closer to the house, and as the English crossed the bridge the Indians fired at them, wounding several (one mortally) before the band could scramble back to the safety of the garrison. In his self-congratulatory memoirs published decades after the war, Church recalled that, after rescuing the mortally wounded man, he stood in the middle and tried to get his comrades to again attack.

At this point, Metacom apparently decided that he had no choice but to go to war against the English. During the next few days, Wampanoag forces attacked Taunton, Rehoboth, and settlements in the surrounding areas, burning abandoned houses and barns, butchering cattle in the fields, and killing colonists when possible. The English were terrorized, not knowing where or when the warriors would hit next, and most abandoned these towns. After carrying out these raids, Metacom had his people evacuate the vulnerable peninsula of Mount Hope for Pocasset territory (a subgroup of the Wampanoag) across the bay on the mainland, near the present-day towns of Tiverton and Fall River. On June 30, when Plymouth troops commanded by Thomas Savage carefully invaded and swept across Mount Hope (on the way passing through the abandoned Kickamuit settlement, where they found the heads and hands of English killed there on June 24), they found abandoned villages but no Wampanoags. Savage decided to build a fort there and patrol the Swansea area, although Church urged that they should immediately pursue Metacom across the bay.

Church's assessment proved astute. While the Pocasset sachem Weetamoo had told Church in early June that she hoped to avoid war, by this time she had agreed to receive Metacom and his warriors in their swampy territory. While the English guarded the abandoned peninsula, Metacom's forces were enlarged by Pocassets and warriors from elsewhere in the area. Nine days later, the Wampanoags attacked Middleborough, near the village of Namasket, where Sassamon had fought. The group was headed by Tispaquin, who was the "Black Sachem" and Metacom's brother-in-law. The warriors looted and burned most of the town as the much smaller garrison of only 17 Englishmen watched. As with Taunton and Rehoboth, Middleborough remained abandoned during the remainder of the war.

THE WAR EXPANDS

Massachusetts followed up on its military assistance by sending diplomatic missions to make sure that other tribes would not join Metacom. Ephraim Curtis led a party to speak with the Nipmucs. He met with 16 sachems on June 24 and 25, who reassured him that none of their men had gone to join Metacom, and that they remained loyal to Massachusetts and considered the war a matter between Metacom and Plymouth. Also on June 25, a delegation led by Edward Hutchinson, son of the famous Puritan exile Anne Hutchinson, met with the Narragansett sachems. Pessicus and Ninigret told the delegates that none of their people had joined Metacom, and they agreed to turn over any Wampanoags who sought refuge—but also expressed their concern that Massachusetts and Rhode Island were seeking to help Plymouth against Metacom. The next day, English fears increased when a hundred armed Narragansetts visited Warwick, Rhode Island. However, the warriors left without incident. Apparently the sachems were either dissembling or had little influence over their men.

Three weeks later, while Metacom and the Wampanoags remained somewhere in the Pocasset area, Curtis escorted Uncas and his Mohegan warriors home from Boston, where they had offered their assistance to the colony. Stopping at a Christian Nipmuc village on July 14, he heard a report that Matoonas, the constable in the "praying town" of Pakachoog, had been seen with 50 Wampanoag warriors. He decided to try to seek negotiations, but encountered a group of angry warriors who nearly shot him and his party before several sachems arrived and, after speaking with Curtis's Natick guides, restored calm. But on the same day, Matoonas and his Nipmucs attacked Mendon, killed four or five colonists working in their fields, and then left. This was the first attack outside Plymouth, the first involving a group other than Wampanoags, and the first led by Christian Indians. The attack led residents to abandon the town, and that winter the Nipmucs returned and burned the empty buildings.

While Metacom's anger is easy to understand, Nipmuc reasons for attacking the English are less clear. Certainly they were concerned about the colonists' intentions. The sachems initially told Curtis that they had heard the English had killed a Nipmuc man in the north, and intended to "destroy them all." A week later some of the sachems informed him that Black James, the Nipmuc Christian constable of Chaubunagungamaug (modern Dudley, Massachusetts), threatened that the English would kill all who were not Christians. For two decades, the "praying towns" had produced Native American missionaries such as Sassamon, who spread English influence, and in 1674 John Eliot and Daniel Gookin traveled through Nipmuc country, putting Native American constables and teachers in charge of various villages. Massachusetts officials also pressured the Nipmucs by negotiating the purchase of land from several sachems, and there were already several Massachusetts Bay Colony settlements in the tribe's territory.

In early July, the colonists received reports that some Wampanoags had found refuge with the Narragansetts, some Narragansetts had joined with the Wampanoags, or that some Narragansetts were independently robbing English homes. Massachusetts and Connecticut sent delegations and troops from Swansea to confront the tribe's sachems and insist that the tribe send hostages to Boston as guarantees of friendship. The conference began around July 11.

The Narragansetts insisted that they were neutral in the conflict, but could not control individuals from their tribe. The English threatened to attack unless they received guarantees of Narragansett friendship, so on July 15 four tribal counselors reluctantly agreed to a treaty. They promised to turn over any of Metacom's people, return all goods stolen from the colonists, release hostages, and recognize all land sales to the English made by their people. But the treaty was meaningless and did more to alienate than secure the tribe, since none of the Narragansett sachems nor war captains were present. Indeed, the Connecticut representatives objected to the Massachusetts Bay Colony's demand for hostages, noting that the tribe was still neutral and should not be treated as enemies.

WAMPANOAGS AND NIPMUCS UNITE

While Massachusetts and Connecticut forces intimidated the Narragansetts, a band of about 36 Plymouth soldiers, including Benjamin Church, tried to do the same to the Pocassets—apparently unaware that Metacom had joined with Weetamoo's people. They stumbled into a large force of Wampanoags and were able to escape only when a sloop suddenly arrived and brought them to safety. Hearing of the battle, Boston authorities ordered the troops returning from Narragansett territory to wait at Taunton and join with Plymouth forces in order to corner Metacom. On July 19, the combined forces entered Pocasset territory. They initially came across a few camps, all abandoned, but as they moved deeper into the swamp they found and then attacked the Wampanoags. The Indians fought off attack after attack, and at the end of the day the English left the swamp, having lost between 5 and 10 men. Those casualties and their failure to strike Metacom's main force led the colonists to change tactics and instead build a fort that would allow them to cut off and starve their enemy.

But Metacom again outfoxed the English. On July 29, he sent warriors to attack and burn Dartmouth. The well-planned assault drew most of the English troops stationed at the fort, allowing Metacom and 63 warriors to escape across the Taunton River and northwest toward Nipmuc territory. Unfortunately, he was forced to leave more than 100 women and children, who were promptly taken by the colonists and sold into slavery. The Wampanoags were then attacked at modern-day Smithfield, Rhode Island, by a 265-man force from Connecticut, including Uncas and his Mohegans, who killed 23 men, including four of Metacom's best leaders. But mistakes by the English allowed the survivors to escape along the Blackstone River. While Weetamoo and a few of her warriors decided to seek refuge with Ninigret, Metacom and his men traveled up into Nipmuc territory and, on August 5, arrived at a fort the tribe had built at Menameset (present-day New Braintree, Massachusetts).

COMPARING THE COMBATANTS

Metacom faced daunting odds against the English. He was without allies and had fewer than 300 men. The English colonies could muster more than 10,000 men and much better supplies. Initially there was no obvious reason for Massachusetts and Connecticut to enter the war, but, as with Plymouth, they had dealt diplomatically with Metacom in the past. While the Rhode Islanders were officially pariahs, the colony's leaders had already shown that they would support their English cousins. Like other northeastern tribes, the Wampanoags were a loosely knit confederation of villages and kinship groups, and Metacom lacked the authority naturally held by an English magistrate or commander.

Yet in the initial stages of the war the Wampanoags had the advantage. Native American men were trained from an early age to stalk game—and their enemies—quietly and patiently. Their goal in warfare was to capture rather than kill, and to do so quickly without losing any of their own, which meant that they favored small, highly mobile groups and independent decision making by band leaders. Their hierarchy was fairly weak and their war leaders gained authority by their ability to guide successful strikes at the enemy with minimum losses to their men.

By contrast, the colonists were farmers and few had real fighting experience. They used the English militia system in which every able-bodied adult male was supposed to be part of a local company, led by local officers often elected by the company, which drilled regularly in maneuvering and firing as a group. Europeans generally emphasized a structured hierarchy and large armies, and the English had developed in Ireland the tactic of building forts as outposts and symbols of dominance where they faced native opposition. This was probably why Thomas Savage decided to build a fort at Mount Hope. These sluggish tactics drew the scorn of Indian warriors, as Mary Rowlandson found out when she was captured at Lancaster, Massachusetts, in January 1676.

> I cannot but remember how the Indians derided the slowness, and dullness of the English army, in its setting out. For after the desolations at Lancaster and Medfield, as I went along with them, they asked me when I thought the English army would come after them? I told them I could not tell: It may be they will come in May, said they. Thus did they scoff at us, as if the English would be a quarter of a year getting ready. Which also I have hinted before, when the English army with new supplies were sent forth to pursue after the enemy, and they understanding it, fled before them till they came to Baquag [Quabaug] river, where they forthwith went over safely: that that river should be impassable to the English.[13]

During this time, both Massachusetts and Connecticut were distracted by other problems. Since the restoration of English king Charles II in 1660, the former had faced a

In 1674, Edmund Andros was appointed governor of New York and New Jersey by James II, the duke of York. During the time of King Philip's War, Andros had designs on claiming the western areas of Massachusetts and Connecticut, and, in fact, would later serve as the governor of the Dominion of New England.

series of threats as the new king sought to reduce or eliminate the Puritan colony's autonomy, and the latter found its western areas claimed by the powerful New York governor Edmund Andros.

Both Indians and English used a mixture of weapons, including muskets and spears. The Wampanoags were skilled with the bow and arrow, which was more dependable than a musket in wet weather, and could be reloaded and fired more quickly and quietly than muskets. Most of the muskets

NATHANIEL SALTONSTALL DESCRIBES ENGLISH LOSSES

Many in England were interested in how their American cousins were faring in the war. In early 1676, Massachusetts leader Nathaniel Saltonstall published in London a brief account that provided details of the sufferings of the colonists but little about Indian grievances or the causes of the war. His lascivious description of warriors raping women would become common in Anglo-American accounts of Indian wars, although personal accounts by Mary Rowlandson and others show this to be a lie. Saltonstall's account is more accurate in showing how the Native Americans targeted the colonists' cattle as symbols of the unwelcome changes that the English brought to their region.

A True but Brief Account of our Losses sustained since this Cruel and Mischievous War began, take as follows.

In Narraganset not One House left standing.

At Warwick but One.

At Providence not above Three.

At Potuxit none left.

Very Few at Seaconicke.

At Swansey two at most.

Marlborough wholly laid ashes, except two or three Houses.

Grantham and Nashaway [Lancaster] all ruined but one house or two.

Many Houses burnt at Springfield, Scituate, Lancaster, Brookefield, and Northampton.

held on both sides were matchlocks. These used a lit string to ignite the gunpowder and were so heavy that a forked pole was used to support the barrel, although the faster and lighter flintlocks were increasingly being used. More of the English owned these weapons, and the Wampanoags were largely

The greatest part of Rehoboth and Taunton destroyed.

Great spoil made at Hadley, Hatfield and Chelmsford.

Deerfield wholly, and Westfield much ruined.

At Sudbury many Houses burnt, and Some at Hingham, Weymouth, and, Braintree.

Besides particular Farms and Plantations, a great Number, not to be reckoned up, wholly laid waste, or very much damnified.

And as to Persons, it is generally thought, that of the English there hath been Lost in all (Men, Women and Children) above Eight Hundred since the War began; of whom many have been destroyed with exquisite Torments and most inhumane barbarities; the Heathen rarely giving Quarter to those that they take, but if they were Women, they first forced them to satisfie their filthy lusts, and then murthered them, either cutting off the head, ripping open the Belly, or skulping the head of skin and hair, and hanging them up as Trophees; wearing mens fingers as bracelets about their Necks, and stripes of their skins which they dresse for Belts: They knockt one Youth of the Head, and laying him for dead, they stead (or skulp'd) his head of skin and hair; After which the boy wonderfully revived, and is now recovered, only he hath nothing but, the dry Skull, neither skin nor hair on his head; Nor have our Cattle escaped the Cruelty of these worse then brute and savage beasts; For what cattle they took they seldom killed outright; or if they did would eat but little of the flesh, but rather cut their bellies, and letting them go severall days, trailing their guts after them, putting out their eyes, or cutting off one leg, &c.[*]

* Nathaniel Saltonstall, *A New and Further Narrative of the State of New England* (London: J.B., 1676), 13–14.

dependent on Dutch and English traders for powder and shot. But the warriors' tactics and knowledge of the terrain more than compensated for this disadvantage.

While the English tried to coax the Indians into open battle, so as to land one decisive blow, the Wampanoags targeted English homes, barns, and cattle in hit-and-run attacks, partially because they were potent symbols of the invaders, and partially because they knew the colonists were dependent on these vulnerable possessions. As the war spread, Metacom's allies would follow these tactics. After burning Medfield, Massachusetts, in February 1676, a literate (probably Christian) Nipmuc left a note that stated: "You must consider the Indians lost nothing but their life; you must lose your fair houses and cattle."[14]

6

The War Spreads
in the Fall

IN THE MEANTIME, THE MASSACHUSETTS DELEGATES who met with the Narragansetts, including Edward Hutchinson, had left Cambridge on July 28, 1675, to try and negotiate a similar agreement with the Nipmucs. Along the way they found village after village deserted: a troubling sign. On August 1, the small party reached Quabaug, near the new settlement of Brookfield, only to find that prominent Nipmuc village also empty. Hutchinson heard that the Nipmucs were gathered at Menameset, and sent Ephraim Curtis and several other men to arrange a meeting. They managed to find several sachems who seemed angry and in a dangerous mood but agreed to meet there early the next morning. But when the delegation traveled to the meeting place, they found no one there. Local Englishmen persuaded Hutchinson to push on and look for the Nipmuc camp, but as the party went single file through a narrow ravine they were attacked in an ambush. Many Nipmuc warriors poured musket fire from the side as others closed in from behind; 20 of the 28 managed to

In August 1675, the Nipmuc tribe attacked the settlement of Brookfield in present-day Massachusetts. The Nipmucs burned the town and local garrison, and several men who left the safety of the garrison were killed.

clamber up a hillside and get away. Hutchinson was among them but would die of his wounds 17 days later.

The survivors sought refuge in a garrison house in Brookfield, where the approximately 80 residents (mostly women and children) joined them to wait for the inevitable attack. Curtis and Henry Young rode east to get help from Marlborough, but soon ran into a warrior band and were forced to return. Nipmuc warriors led by the Quabaug sachem Muttawmp soon arrived, burned the rest of the town, and besieged the garrison. Several Englishmen who exposed themselves or left the garrison were killed; the besiegers cut off the head of one and used it as a football. Finally, that evening, Curtis managed to make his way past the warriors and ran the 30 miles to Marlborough; the town then sent a messenger to alert Captain Simon Willard at Lancaster about the siege. In the meantime, the Indians tried various tactics to take the house, using flaming arrows to try and set fire to its roof, and then piling hay against a corner of the building to ignite the garrison. In both cases, the besieged managed to put out the fires. Then the warriors tried igniting a large barrel on wheels and using long poles to push it against the house, but a fortuitous rainstorm extinguished the fire. Finally, on August 4, Willard's force arrived and the Nipmucs withdrew. After a few weeks, Willard withdrew his men and took with him the remaining townspeople. Brookfield remained abandoned for nearly two decades.

Shortly after the Nipmucs ended their attack, Metacom arrived at Menameset. The news apparently drew more Native American men into the war. Subsequent operations often (but not always) featured Wampanoag and Nipmuc troops, led by their own sachems but working together for a common goal. The first joint Nipmuc–Wampanoag operation was an attack on Lancaster led by the Nipmuc sachem Monoco on August 22. They managed to burn one house and to kill seven colonists. The English were particularly shocked by this attack, and many suspected that Christian

Indians (including Pennacooks from Wamesit) were also involved. Rumors also reported Metacom near Stonington (in modern-day Connecticut, just west of the Rhode Island border) and at Quabaug, near Brookfield. But the main focus of English fears lay farther west, in the upper Connecticut River Valley.

THE WAR MOVES WEST

The Pocumtuck villages scattered throughout the Connecticut valley, often alongside the colonial settlements, were linked by kinship, language, and shared interests. Leaders of the United Colonies feared that the war would spread into this area, and sent Massachusetts and Connecticut militia and Mohegan allies to the area to help protect settlements. Unfortunately, the colonists' fears caused them to create the very situation they hoped to avoid. When Hatfield authorities heard of the outbreak of the war, they first demanded that the neighboring Pocumtucks surrender their firearms, but soon returned the weapons in order to gain the Indians' assistance against the Quabaugs who attacked Brookfield. But on August 24, acting in part because of rumors from the Mohegans (who had often clashed with the Pocumtucks), and partly due to their own suspicions that the Indians had held back from shooting at their Quabaug relatives, they again demanded the Pocumtucks' weapons. That night, the Indians fled. The next day, captains Thomas Lathrop and Richard Beers led their men in pursuit, but at Hopewell Swamp (present-day Whately, Massachusetts) they were confronted by the Pocumtucks' rear guard. The Indians stopped the English pursuit and killed nine before heading north. The primary result of this incident was to turn a neutral tribe into a firm enemy of the English and to alarm if not alienate other Pocumtuck villages.

On September 1, a large Native American force attacked the town of Deerfield, in the northwestern part of modern-day Massachusetts, killing a man and burning several houses. The next day, warriors surprised and killed eight men at Squakeag (present-day Northfield, Massachusetts) who were working in the woods, and destroyed houses, barns, and crops in the area. One day later, Beers went upriver from Hatfield with a company of about 35 men to evacuate Squakeag. On September 4, about two miles from that town, they walked into an ambush. Beers and about half of his men were killed, and the survivors fled in small groups back to Hatfield. Two days after that deadly encounter, Major Robert Treat and the Connecticut militia in the upper valley evacuated Squakeag, during the course of which they found the heads of some of Beers's men mounted on poles.

Six days later, on September 12, Deerfield was again hit, and the local commanders decided to evacuate. Six days after that, Native American warriors, probably Nipmucs led by Muttawmp, launched an effective attack on Lathrop's company at Muddy Brook, just south of Deerfield, as the English were leaving the town for Northampton. The warriors killed many and destroyed carts full of the colonists' belongings. They decided to withdraw from the attack when troops in the vicinity, led by Moseley, arrived and counterattacked. But the Indian warriors remained in the area, and that night taunted Moseley and his men who holed up in abandoned Deerfield, waving the clothing of militiamen they had killed. The next day the warriors withdrew, allowing Moseley to return to the site of the battle and bury the 64 English dead, including Lathrop. The Battle of Bloody Brook, as the English called it, would become known as the worst disaster to befall the colonists during the war.

By September 22, as the United Colonies raised a force of 500 men to protect western Massachusetts, only five colonial settlements remained in that section of the colony. The largest of these was Springfield, owned and operated by John Pynchon, the fur trader, land speculator, and landlord who for decades

Fought on September 12, 1675, the Battle of Bloody Brook was the most devastating conflict for the English colonists during King Philip's War. Sixty-four Englishmen were killed, including Captain Thomas Lathrop, the commander of the regiment.

had dealt closely with Native Americans in the region. Against his own recommendation, Pynchon was placed in charge of the colonial forces in the valley. The Pocumtucks near Springfield, led by the sachem Wequogan, had agreed to be supervised by a few English elites in order to ensure that more suspicious locals would leave them alone. On September 26, those suspicions increased when a group of unidentified Native Americans burned Pynchon's mill and a few nearby buildings south of the modern Massachusett–Connecticut border. The residents of Springfield were alarmed, but town leaders kept tempers soothed.

On October 4, all of the troops stationed in Springfield headed for Hadley to join with Moseley's forces in a large-scale attack against Native American forces thought to be near that town. That evening, word reached Springfield from Windsor that a local Indian had told them that several hundred hostile warriors had arrived at the Pocumtuck village. Springfield residents went on alert, and Lieutenant Thomas Cooper and several others went the next morning to investigate the rumors. Before reaching the village the men were attacked, apparently by Nipmuc and Pocumtuck warriors led by Wequogan. Cooper was badly wounded, but managed to make it back to Springfield to gasp a warning before dying. The warriors then hit the town, burning more than 300 unoccupied houses while besieging the garrisoned dwellings. In the meantime, the Springfield forces then in Hadley were returning and militia from Westfield led by Treat were on the way. Both arrived that afternoon, at which point the Indians withdrew, leaving behind a devastated town but only one Englishwoman killed and three or four residents wounded.

After the debacle at Springfield, Samuel Appleton of Ipswich replaced Pynchon as regional commander, much to the latter's relief, and Captain Samuel Mosely's forces added their aggressive tactics. Perhaps as a result, the tide of Native American victories and English setbacks seemed to slow. On October 19, warriors led by Quabaug sachem Muttawmp attacked Hatfield, one of the few villages left in the valley, but found the town well defended by Mosely's troops and decided to withdraw rather than risk high casualties for few gains. This was the first time that Native Americans were repulsed before they could do any damage, and the English celebrated it as a turning point. But this was not the end of Indian effectiveness in the valley. Toward the end of the month, warriors from various tribes separately and together raided Northampton on October 25 and 29, killing two residents and burning four houses. On October 26 they hit Westfield, killing three residents and destroying several homes. By mid-November, the colonists were so dispirited that Appleton had to bar them from leaving any of the five remaining valley towns without his permission. But the Indians as well as the English were preparing for winter, and the former made no additional attacks on the latter in the valley that year.

THE WAR EXPANDS TO THE NORTH

Two distinct groupings of Native Americans lived in the region that became Vermont, New Hampshire, and Maine. Those in Maine are Wabanakis ("dawn land people") and those in New Hampshire and Vermont, with a distinctly different dialect, are generally called Western Abenakis. Both groups lived in settlements that were generally distinguished by the rivers and streams along which they lived. South to north, the Wabanaki tribes were the Pigwackets (who lived near the upper Saco and Presumpscot rivers), Androscoggins, Kennebecs, and Penobscots. Western Abenakis were generally divided into Pennacooks, Sokokis, Cowasucks, and Missisquois. All made their livings mostly by hunting, fishing, and gathering, although those who lived in villages along the coast and in more southerly river valleys did raise crops. All of these tribes joined in short-term alliances of villages and families that often broke apart and reformed in new and, for colonists, confusing ways. When war threatened, families and even entire villages would abandon their territories and move to safety, returning months or even years later, and sometimes finding new homes elsewhere.

Coastal New Hampshire and Maine had rich resources—fish, fur, timber, and land—and were early attractions for English investors, colonists, and governments. In the 1620s and 1630s, Plymouth Colony, Massachusetts Bay Colony, and various English and French commercial groups all claimed important sites for trading posts and settlements in this region. Indian deeds became important bargaining chips to key trading posts and real estate. Massachusetts gained dominance in the 1640s and 1650s, displacing Plymouth and English land companies, but the colonial outposts in Maine generally operated beyond the reach of Boston's authority. Since neither Wabanaki nor colonial leaders could command their people—among the Wabanakis by custom, among the English by disregard of custom—reprisals and violence took place in a seemingly unorganized and unpredictable fashion. This lawless situation generated conflict between Native Americans and colonists that would explode with King Philip's War.

When news of the attack on Swansea reached the village of York (in present-day Maine), residents mustered their militia and marched to the Androscoggin village at the Sheepscot River to demand that the Indians surrender their weapons. The Androscoggins were led by Mugg Hegone, who was fluent in English. The members of the village consulted their friends and considered the situation, and decided instead to go on the offensive. The Sacos (who lived along the lower Saco River in southwestern Maine) were already angered by the fraud and violence perpetrated by English traders and colonists. A frequently told story is that, shortly before the war began, the wife and infant son of their sachem Squando were canoeing down the Saco River when they were seized by English sailors. Local lore held that Indian children could swim at birth, and the sailors decided to test the idea by throwing Squando's son into Casco Bay, proving folklore incorrect and forever making an enemy of the sachem.

On September 5, a Saco band raided Thomas Purchase's trading post on the Pejebscot River, where the modern town of Topsham is located, looting the house and killing some cattle but leaving the Purchase family unharmed—although they threatened that others would soon come and do worse. Four days later, three Penobscots knocking on the door of an English home on the north shore of Casco Bay were fired on by a passing party of Englishmen, who were no doubt on edge because of the general hostilities. One was killed and one wounded. Fortunately for the English, the Penobscots decided not to seek revenge and instead headed north out of harm's way.

But the Sacos, Androscoggins, and other Wabanaki warriors launched a series of effective attacks on various settlements along Casco Bay and farther south. On September 12,

Thomas Wakely's house at Falmouth (present-day Portland) was hit; the raiders burned the house and killed Thomas, his wife, and three of their grandchildren, and took 11-year-old Elizabeth Wakely as the first captive in the war. Other English in the area ran south to take refuge in Major William Philip's garrison house on the west side of the Saco River. On September 18, a large war band burned John Bonython's home on the east side of the Saco and then attacked Philip's place, burning his mills and nearly taking the garrison house. In mid-September, Wabanakis also attacked the settlement at Oyster River (present-day Durham, New Hampshire), burning two houses, killing two settlers, and capturing another; a few days later, they killed five English along the Saco River. The colonists abandoned Winter Harbor, and when a company of militia landed there they were hit hard, with more than a dozen killed.

Beginning in late September, the Androscoggins began raiding York and nearby towns. On October 1, they attacked Richard Tozer's house (in what is now Berwick, Maine); most in the structure fled, but Tozer and his son remained and for their stubbornness were killed in another attack two weeks later. A few days after the death of the Tozers, Roger Plaisted and two of his sons were killed defending a neighboring garrison. The Wabanakis left, spreading destruction and death on their way home. Another war band hit Black Point (Scarborough, Maine), destroying seven homes and killing several settlers. Finally, Wabanakis raided Wells, Maine, killing three and burning a house. As the month ended, the Native Americans scattered for their winter villages, leaving 80 colonists dead, many houses burned, and the English tide of expansion blunted.

Uncertain Allies and New Enemies

INDIAN SUPPORT FOR THE WAR WAS NOT UNIVERSAL. THE Mohegans were close allies of the English. On July 15, at the outbreak of the war, the Mohegans and Pequots who had joined them after the Pequot War both readily swore their loyalty and provided warriors for the United Colonies. In September, the Niantics, who held close kinship relations with the Narragansetts, pledged their "fidelity and good affection" for the English.[15] In addition, precolonial tribal bonds had been weakened by the new Christian networks and by political connections with the English. The Massachusett tribe, some Pennacooks, and a number of Nipmucs and Wampanoags refused to join Metacom, and many men in the older Eliot praying towns asked to join colonial forces.

Despite their loyalty, most colonists blamed all Indians for the revolt and believed that they were all enemies. In August 1675, as the war grew more intense, the Massachusetts Bay Colony confined all friendly Indians to a few easterly praying towns. Colonists confiscated or destroyed property in various Christian Indian communities, including crops and tools, and threatened to kill the defenseless Native Americans. In early September, the Niantic sachem Ninigret sent eight ambassadors to Boston to negotiate his visit; on their way out of town, two Englishmen grabbed one, accusing him of having fought with Metacom. The Indian man was hung two days later. Still, Ninigret was persuaded to come to Boston, where Massachusetts Bay Colony leaders told him that he had to surrender the Pocasset "Squaw Sachem" Weetamoo, who had joined Metacom and then fled to the Narragansetts after the swamp fight. Although Ninigret managed to get out of town safely, the chaos of the war (if not his own preferences) kept him from meeting that demand.

As the war expanded and became more dangerous, Massachusetts Bay Colony authorities became more sympathetic to the burgeoning hostility toward the Christian Indians. In October, the Nipmucs in Okommakamesit were marched to jail in Boston when the residents of adjoining Marlborough accused them of participating in Metacom's attacks; they were released after several days and sent to Natick. When a haystack was burned in Chelmsford, the court ordered the arrest of the men in nearby Wamesit and distant Punkapoag; the latter were released after a quick interrogation, but the Wamesits suffered a long period of imprisonment in Boston. After those imprisoned were released and returned to Wamesit, Chelmsford men burned their homes and crops and killed women, children, and elderly men. The survivors hurried to join Pennacook sachem Wannalancet, who with many of his tribe had fled earlier to avoid the conflict. Finally, on October 30, when a shack burned in Dedham, the nearby Natick Indians were sent to Deer Island in Boston Harbor. The Christian Indians were also harassed by their Native American cousins. In early November, a large group of Nipmuc warriors entered a Christian Nipmuc camp east of Brookfield and forced them or convinced them to join their side.

By February 1676, the Indian population incarcerated on Deer Island swelled to 550, as the Punkapoags were sent there in December and the Nashobas arrived in February after spending several months locked in a house in Concord. The inhabitants on the wind-swept bit of rock were "in want of all things almost, except clams, which food (as some conceived) did occasion fluxes and other diseases among them; besides, they were very mean for clothing, and the Island were bleak and cold with the sea winds in spring time, and the place afforded little fuel, and their wigwams were mean." Despite English hostility and abuse, Indian men on the island clamored to help in the war against Metacom, perhaps showing their deep loyalty to the Christian colony, a long-standing dislike of the Wampanoags, or maybe due to a strong desire to escape the poor conditions on the island. When the General Court finally approved native enlistment, about 100 Indian men contributed their critical scouting skills to the colonial effort. Those who remained on the island depended on the little food brought by John Eliot.[16]

Ironically, the safest place for Indians in the region was probably the Wampanoag village of Mashpee in Plymouth Colony. The town had been set aside in the 1660s for Christian Indians in the area, and at the outbreak of the war Plymouth required all Indians on Cape Cod to live there during the conflict. Similarly, the Wampanoags on the islands of Martha's Vineyard and Nantucket swore their loyalty to the English at the beginning of the war, which was fortunate for the English because the Wampanoags outnumbered the colonists on those islands 20 to 1. The settlers on Martha's Vineyard discussed forcing the Aquinnahs on the western side of the island to surrender their weapons, but after negotiating with the community agreed that it was best to set them up as a guard against Metacom's warriors, which proved quite effective at least in keeping the peace.

ENTER THE NARRAGANSETTS

In the 1660s and early 1670s, the Narragansett tribe insisted on its sovereignty even as the United Colonies became increasingly adamant about controlling the region. When the war broke out, the tribe tried to remain neutral despite decades of still-smoldering resentments toward Massachusetts and Connecticut, probably because they were divided between the younger war hawks who wished to join Metacom against the arrogant Puritans and those who followed the more cautious elder sachems.

On October 11, 1675, Roger Williams met with Canonchet, a young Narragansett sachem, and warned him that Metacom was irrational and would lose the war and that the English would destroy any who helped him. A week later, the tribe agreed with the United Colonies to continue the peace and by October 28 turn over any Wampanoags who sought refuge with them. Eleven days after that, Ninigret agreed to the same terms with Connecticut. Other, smaller Native American groups living in close proximity to the English must have been particularly desperate to avoid appearing hostile. Two Connecticut River tribes, the Wongunk and "Nayags," negotiated an agreement that placed Uncas's son—whom the colonists trusted—in charge.

But for decades the "orthodox" Puritans had suspected the Narragansetts of duplicity and that tribe in turn had many reasons to be angry at the Puritans' overbearing actions. It is entirely likely that, despite the protestations of Canonchet and other tribal leaders, many Narragansett warriors would have joined the fight against the Puritans. Pessicus had even admitted as much to Williams when the war began, and as the deadline to turn over Wampanoags approached, tribal leaders made it clear that they would not. The extensive kinship networks and family loyalties that had given the tribe much of its power for decades now prevented its members

On December 19, 1675, a United Colonial force of more than 1,000 men, along with 150 Mohegans and Pequots, attacked the Narragansetts' main village in Rhode Island (at present-day South Kingston) in what came to be known as the Great Swamp Fight. The English forces burned the settlement and approximately 600 Narragansetts, mostly women and children, died in the blaze.

from turning over Wampanoags or hostages. But regardless of whether the Narragansetts met that deadline, the United Colonies would not allow the tribe to remain neutral given their potential threat (and the attraction of their land). Therefore, in mid-November, the United Colonies decided to take preemptive action.

On December 9, about 600 Massachusetts Bay Colony militia members left Dedham and headed for Rhode Island. Along the way they were joined by 150 Plymouth troops. Plymouth governor Josiah Winslow led the army. On December 18, they met up with Connecticut forces led by Robert Treat, who commanded 300 Englishmen and 150 Mohegans and Pequots. The next day, this army, guided through the swamps by a Narragansett man, quietly encircled the very large, fortified Narragansett "capital" (present-day South Kingston) and launched an attack with the hope of destroying the tribe altogether, as their fathers had done to the Pequots in 1637. A daylong battle later known as the Great Swamp Fight ensued, during which the English set fire to the village. Large numbers of warriors slipped out during the battle so that most of the 600 Narragansetts who died in the cataclysm were women and children. The army of the United Colonies was badly mauled in the siege, with 34 killed and about 50 mortally wounded, and was unable to pursue the Narragansetts who had escaped. Those warriors brought an intense desire for revenge to the swelling forces that would challenge the English.

WINTER DEVASTATIONS

The rest of December and early January was unusually cold, and combatants from both sides focused on staying warm in their homes. There was one exception: Metacom, with about 400 of his warriors, was traveling to Schaghticoke on the Hudson River to meet with the Mohawks in an effort to gain their support against the English. The Mohawks were the most feared warriors in the Northeast and were the traditional enemies of Native American peoples in southern New England, but Metacom hoped that they would share his desire to reduce, if not end, the aggressive and growing strength of the Puritan colonists. Unfortunately for Metacom and the Indian fight for sovereignty, the Mohawks had already received a message from Sir Edmund Andros, governor of New York, seeking to strengthen his alliance with that tribe and asking as a personal favor for them to attack Metacom. They were happy to do so. Almost all of Metacom's men were killed, and the survivors retreated east.

In the meantime, a January thaw allowed the Indians to again attack colonial outposts. On January 27, the Narragansetts emerged from a hidden camp in the Rhode Island swamps and attacked Pawtuxet (parts of present-day Cranston and Warwick), burning buildings and stealing livestock, and then headed off to join the Nipmucs and others camped along the slope of Mount Wachusett in central Massachusetts. A United Colonies force of 1,400, led by Winslow, followed to try and bring the Narragansetts to open battle, but the Native Americans knew the territory too well. A series of costly skirmishes and lack of preparation left the militia discouraged and near starvation. On February 3, Winslow abandoned the chase and brought his troops to Boston. Once at Wachusett, Canonchet, the young Narragansett sachem who led the defense of the tribe's village, apparently became the most influential war leader.

At the end of January, the Christian Nipmuc scout James Quannapohit returned to report to Massachusetts authorities that the warriors at Wachusett planned to raid five settlements on the edges of the colony: Lancaster, Groton, Marlborough, Sudbury, and Medfield. But the English mistrusted Quannapohit and dismissed his report. On February 1, 1676, Nipmucs attacked the garrison of Thomas Eames (present-day Framingham, Massachusetts), killing the wife and several children of the trader, who was not home at the time. Perhaps as a result of this feint, Lancaster was completely unguarded. On February 9, Job Kattenanit returned from Wachusett, going directly to Daniel Gookin's home to warn of the impending attack on Lancaster. The next morning, Monoco, who had attacked the town the previous August, and about 400 warriors hit Lancaster, burning many houses and taking the garrisoned home of village minister Joseph Rowlandson. Several in the garrison were killed but most (24) were taken captive, including Rowlandson's wife, Mary. The warriors withdrew when a relief force arrived.

Mary Rowlandson and the other captives were taken to the warriors' camp at Wachusett, where she was purchased from Monoco by the Narragansett sachem Quinapin. In 1682,

Rowlandson would publish an account of her three-month captivity among the Indians, which focused on her self-absorbed religious musings, but also contained useful observations of

MARY ROWLANDSON DESCRIBES THE ATTACK ON LANCASTER

In 1682, Mary Rowlandson published her account of her capture and captivity among the Nipmucs and Narragansetts during the war. *The Sovereignty and Goodness of God* created a pattern copied by many subsequent "captivity narratives," including inexplicably savage actions of Indian attackers and the manner in which good and bad events were manifestations of a higher meaning rather than random occurrences or the results of plans made by the Indians. Rowlandson's description of the destruction of her town and the deaths of family members is one of the more evocative accounts of losses from the war.

On the tenth of February 1676, came the Indians with great numbers upon Lancaster: Their first coming was about sun-rising; hearing the noise of some guns, we looked out; several houses were burning, and the smoke ascending to heaven. . . .

Some in our house were fighting for their lives, others wallowing in their blood, the house on fire over our heads, and the bloody heathen ready to knock us on the head, if we stirred out. . . . But out we must go, the fire increasing, and coming along behind us, roaring, and the Indians gaping before us with their guns, spears and hatchets to devour us. No sooner were we out of the house, but my brother-in-law (being before wounded, in defending the house, in or near the throat) fell down dead whereat the Indians scornfully shouted, and holloed, and were presently upon him, stripping off his clothes, the bullets flying thick, one went through my side, and the same (as would seem)

Native American life and customs, of political meetings and negotiations between the Indians and the English, and of her meetings with Metacom after he returned from New York.

through the bowels and hand of my dear child in my arms . . . Thus were we butchered by those merciless heathen, standing amazed, with the blood running down to our heels. My eldest sister being yet in the house, and seeing those woeful sights, the infidels haling mothers one way, and children another, and some wallowing in their blood: and her elder son telling her that her son William was dead, and myself was wounded, she said, And, Lord, let me die with them; which was no sooner said, but she was struck with a bullet, and fell down dead over the threshold. . . . the Indians laid hold of us, pulling me one way, and the Children another, and said, Come go along with us; I told them they would kill me: they answered, If I were willing to go along with them, they would not hurt me.

Oh the doleful sight that now was to behold at this house! Come, behold the works of the Lord, what desolations he has made in the earth . . . It is solemn sight to see so many Christians lying in their blood, some here, and some there, like a company of sheep torn by wolves. All of them stripped naked by a company of hell-hounds, roaring singing, ranting and insulting, as if they would have torn of very hearts out; yet the Lord by his almighty power preserved number of us from death, for there were twenty-four of us taken alive and carried captive. . . .

Now away we must go with those barbarous creatures, with of bodies wounded and bleeding, and our hearts no less than of bodies . . . This was the dolefullest night that ever my eyes saw. Oh, the roaring, and singing and dancing, and yelling of those black creatures in the night, which made the place a lively resemblance of hell*

---

* Mary Rowlandson, *The Sovereignty and Goodness of God* (Boston, 1682), reprinted in *So Dreadful a Judgment: Puritan Responses to King Philip's War, 1676–1677*, Richard Slotkin and James K. Folsom, eds. (Middletown, Conn.: Wesleyan University Press, 1978), 323–326.

On February 10, 1676, Monoco and approximately 400 Narragansett and Nipmuc warriors attacked the English settlement of Lancaster in present-day Massachusetts. Although some residents were killed during the attack, the majority (24) were taken prisoner, including Mary Rowlandson, the village minister's wife. Rowlandson is depicted here being taken to the Narragansetts' camp at Wachusett.

She had a good relationship with many of the enemy warriors but was abused by her master's spouse, the "squaw sachem" Weetamoo. Rowlandson's *The Sovereignty and Goodness of God* was the first colonial account of Indian captivity, and became a prototype for a huge body of American literature.

Lancaster was abandoned in the wake of the attack. Next it was Medfield's turn. After midnight on February 21, 300 Nipmucs and Narragansetts infiltrated the town despite the nearly 100 troops stationed there, and began shooting the inhabitants as they emerged in the morning. The Indians burned the town, killed about 18 people and took large numbers captive. Thomas Thurston's wife fled her lodgings at a friend's house when the attack began; she was hit or fell and appeared dead to the Indians, so "they stript her [naked] & tooke of[f] her head cloths." She regained consciousness, grabbed a blanket as cover, and ran to a neighbor's house— but her bloody, naked appearance was such "a frightfull spectacle" that they did not recognize her.[17] A Christian Nipmuc who took part in the raid left a note boasting that they would soon be in Boston. That seemed prophetic: four days later, a raiding party burned buildings in Weymouth along the coast, just south of Boston. Groton was raided March 2 and 9, and hit in force by Monoco's Nipmucs on March 13. It was abandoned. Three days later, Indian forces burned all but one (stone) house in Warwick, Rhode Island.

On March 12, a band led by Totson attacked William Clark's garrison on the Eel River, several miles south of Plymouth, killing Clark, his wife, and their nine children. Increase Mather, a Boston minister and one of the most prominent men in New England, wrote that Clark's wife was "the Daughter of a godly Father and Mother that came to *New England* on the account of Religion, and she herself also a pious and prudent Woman." The leader of the attack "was one *Totoson*, a fellow who was well acquainted with that house, and had received many kindnesses there, it being the manner of those bruitish men, who are only skilful to destroy, to deal worst with those who have done most for them." Mather also wrote angrily that the Nipmucs who attacked Groton on March 13 burned first "the *House of God*," and then went to Reverend Willard's garrison house and "scoffed and blasphemed . . . and tauntingly, said, *What will you do for a house to pray in now we have burnt your Meeting-house?* Thus hath the Enemy done wickedly in the Sanctuary, they have burnt up the Synagogues of God in the Land; they have cast fire into the Sanctuary; they have cast down the dwelling place of his name to the Ground."[18] Such episodes outraged colonial authorities and for them justified giving captured Indians no quarter.

Farther from the coast, a United Colonies force marching west from Brookfield and targeting Menameset was unable to find anyone to fight and wound up in Hadley. But the Pocumtucks and others were out there, and on March 14, they again hit Northampton, killing five people and burning 10 houses before the militia led by Robert Treat and William Turner drove them off. This was the only skirmish in the western part of Massachusetts in the late spring, and in early April a group of soldiers from the Boston area returned to their homes. The lull in the war in this area allowed Native Americans in the Connecticut River Valley to return to their villages to plant, fish, and replenish their supplies.

In eastern Massachusetts and Plymouth, the series of devastating winter attacks drove large numbers of refugees into Boston: abandoned (in addition to the towns noted above) were Dartmouth, Rehoboth, Swansea, Wrentham, Mendon, and Groton, all in Massachusetts, in addition to Simsbury, Connecticut. Colonists began to see hostile Indians everywhere. The resulting drain on resources, social conflicts, and paranoia handicapped their defense. After residents of Andover and Haverhill in the north reported sighting Native Americans in the area, Massachusetts moved troops into those towns. Instead, on March 26, one band

MARY ROWLANDSON'S
MEETING WITH METACOM

The casting by Mary Rowlandson of her captivity in Biblical terms illustrates how English Puritans tended to interpret events; her description of smoking illuminates how the Indians and the English shared many customs at this time; and the way in which she readily made a shirt for Metacom's son reflects her unthinking acceptance of gender roles even in the enemy camp. This is also the last description of Metacom before his death in the summer of 1676.

Although I had met with so much affliction, and my heart was many times ready to break, yet could I not shed one tear in their sight: but rather had been all this while in a maze, and like one astonished: but now I may say as, Psalm 137. 1. By the rivers of Babylon, there we sat down: yea, we wept when we remembered Zion. There one of them asked me, why I wept, I could hardly tell what to say: yet I answered, they would kill me: No, said he, none will hurt you. Then came one of them and gave me two spoonfuls of meal to comfort me, and another gave me half a pint of peas; which was more worth than many bushels at another time. Then I went to see King Philip, he bade me come in and sit down, and asked me whether I would smoke (a usual compliment nowadays amongst saints and sinners) but this no way suited me. For though I had formerly used tobacco, yet I had left it ever since I was first taken. It seems to be a bait, the devil lays to make men lose their precious time: I remember with shame, how formerly, when I had taken two or three pipes, I was presently ready for another, such a bewitching thing it is: but I thank God, he has now given me power over it; surely there are many who may be better employed than to lie sucking a stinking tobacco pipe. . . .

(continues)

(continued)

During my abode in this place, Philip spake to me to make a shirt for his boy, which I did, for which he gave me a shilling: I offered the money to my master but he bade me keep it: and with it I bought a piece of horse flesh. Afterwards he asked me to make a cap for his boy, for which he invited me to dinner. I went, and he gave me a pancake, about as big as two fingers; it was made of parched wheat, beaten, and fried in bear's grease, but I thought I never tastes pleasanter meat in my life. There was a squaw who spake to me to make a shirt for her sannup [husband], for which she gave me a piece of bear. Another asked me to knit a pair of stockings, for which she gave me a quart of peas: I boiled my peas and bear together, and invited my master and mistress to dinner, but the proud gossip because I served them both in one dish, would eat nothing, except one bit that he gave her upon the point of his knife.*

* Mary Rowlandson, *The Sovereignty and Goodness of God* (Boston, 1682), reprinted in *So Dreadful a Judgment: Puritan Responses to King Philip's War, 1676–1677,* Richard Slotkin and James K. Folsom, eds. (Middletown, Conn.: Wesleyan University Press, 1978), 336–337.

raided Longmeadow, much farther west and south, killing two and taking four captive, and another band hit Marlborough, burning 11 barns and 13 homes. Marlborough was abandoned (although soldiers used it as a base) and another group of warriors burned the abandoned town of Simsbury.

The War Seesaws, Spring and Summer 1676

THE INDIANS' SUCCESSFUL RAIDS CONTINUED AS WINTER gave way to spring. On March 26 at Central Falls on the Pawtucket River, Narragansett warriors successfully ambushed a Plymouth militia company that was searching for them, killing 42 of the 63 men. Two days later, Canonchet's band attacked Old Rehoboth, burning a large number of barns and homes, a sawmill, and two grinding mills. The following day the same band laid waste to Providence—but Canonchet and other warriors first met with his old friend Roger Williams. Williams asked him "Why they assaulted us With burning and Killing who ever were [kind?] Neighbours to them (and looking back) said I this Hous[e] of mine now burning before mine Eyes hath Lodged kindly Some Thousands of You these Ten Years." They told him that Rhode Island had joined forces with Massachusetts and Plymouth. Williams replied that his colony had behaved peaceably, but that they were "like Wolves tearing, and Devouring the Innocent."[19]

A strange theological and political debate ensued between Williams and the Narragansetts as Providence burned in the background. The Indians "Confessed they were in A Strang Way. 2ly we had forced them to it. 3ly that God was [with] them and Had forsaken us for they had so prospered in Killing and Burning us far beyond What we did against them." Williams bitterly taunted them that they were wrong, for "God had prospered us so that wee had driven the Wampanoogs with Phillip out of his Countrie and the Nahigonsiks out of their Countrie and had destroyed Multitudes of them in Fighting and Flying, In Hungr and Cold etc.: and that God would help us to Consume them." Yet even after Williams again met and upbraided the attackers, they parted with surprising amity. He noted that "they were so Civill that they called after me and bid me not go near the Burned Houses for their might be Indians [that] might mischief me, but goe by the Water Side."[20]

The devastating attacks continued. On April 9, warriors hit Bridgewater, near Swansea, burning a house and a barn and destroying food stores. Six days later, a band burned Chelmsford (which had been abandoned) in the north; two days after that, a different group destroyed the buildings that remained in Marlborough, west of Boston. Swiftly moving warriors killed settlers and burned buildings in Andover, Hingham, Weymouth, Haverhill, Hadley, Worcester, Mendon, Wrentham, Medfield, Billerica, Braintree, and Woburn. The English tried to hit back. After Marlborough was burned on April 17, a militia company pursued the attackers and managed to attack their camp that night. But most of the time the colonial soldiers found themselves under siege and unable to respond effectively.

On April 21, about 500 warriors led by Muttawmp attacked Sudbury, 17 miles west of Boston, burning homes and besieging garrisons to which the soldiers as well as settlers retreated. Several companies rushed to the battle, which went on all day: 60 from Concord, who were trapped and all slaughtered; those from Marlborough, 30 of whom were killed; and troops from Charlestown and from Brookfield. Between May 8 and May 20, three towns in southeastern

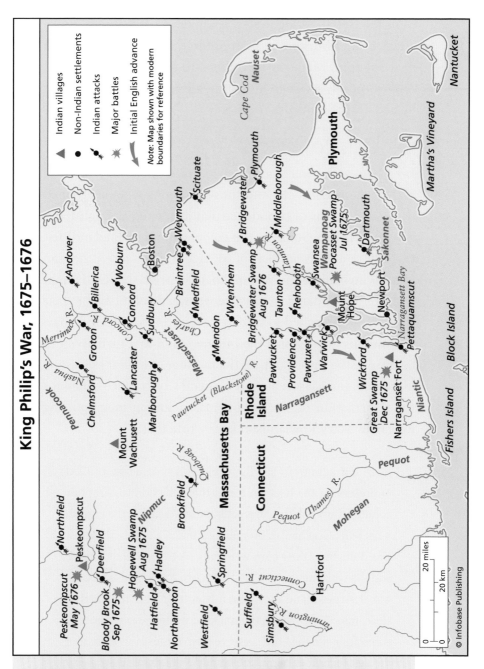

The major battles of King Philip's War are depicted on this map, including Bloody Brook (in present-day western Massachusetts) and Great Swamp (in present-day southern Rhode Island). By April 1676, Indian forces had reached Boston's doorstep, burning buildings in the towns of Braintree, Weymouth, and Woburn.

Massachusetts—Bridgewater, Halifax, and Scituate—were attacked and burned by a large force (about 300 men) led by Tispaquin, Metacom's brother-in-law and the sachem of Assawompset, a village in that area that before the war had hosted a Christian congregation.

ENGLISH CONFLICTS

Even before the war, the colonists were divided by political and religious conflicts, and those divisions were sharpened by an acute crisis of confidence that deepened as English defeats multiplied. Some in the colonies (and in England) felt that Plymouth's treatment of Metacom had caused the war. Many who blamed the Wampanoags worried that God might be using the Indians to chastise wayward colonists for their sins. Plymouth called a fast day for June 24 to seek God's pardon and his help against the Indians—and that turned out to be the day the war began. As the number of military disasters increased, the Massachusetts General Court twice called for the reformation of a series of sins, including men sporting long hair. Mary Rowlandson later wrote that:

> I can but admire to see the wonderful providence of God in preserving the heathen for further affliction to our poor country. They could go in great numbers over, but the English must stop: God had an overruling hand in all those things. It was thought, if their corn were cut down, they would starve and die with hunger: and all their corn that could be found, was destroyed, and they driven from that little they had in store, into the woods in the midst of winter; and yet how to admiration did the Lord preserve them for his Holy ends, and the destruction of many still amongst the English! Strangely did the Lord provide for them; that I did not see (all the time I w. among them) one man, woman, or child, die with hunger. Though many times they would eat that, that a hog or a do would hardly touch; yet by that God strengthened them to be

scourge to His people. . . . our perverse and evil carriages in the sight of the Lord, have so offended Him, that instead of turning His hand against them, the Lord feeds and nourishes them up to be a scourge to the whole Land.[21]

Ironically, while many in Massachusetts also wondered whether the war was God's punishment for becoming too tolerant of Quakers and other religious dissidents, those Quakers (especially the large number in Rhode Island) were happy to point out that the Indians' successes were God's justice for the Puritans' past and present persecution of dissenters. They protested the violations of their territory by troops of the United Colonies, and their protests (along with those of others) reached

John Eliot, depicted here preaching to a group of Native Americans, was a Puritan missionary who translated the Bible into the Algonquian language—the first Bible printed in North America. During King Philip's War, Eliot was accused of being an Indian sympathizer and was nearly lynched in Boston for attempting to ferry supplies to the Christian Indians who lived on Deer Island.

sympathetic ears in England. Royal authorities in England were already reviewing the laws and actions of Massachusetts, with an eye toward curbing or ending that colony's autonomy.

As the colonists suffered more losses, they began to turn on each other. On January 14, 1676, Joshua Tift was captured near Providence and charged with having become a renegade. He admitted to being with the Narragansetts when the English attacked in the Great Swamp Fight, but denied helping the enemy. His plea of duress was rejected, and he was found guilty of treason and executed. John Eliot and Daniel Gookin were nearly lynched by Bostonians in the winter when they sought to ferry supplies over to the Christian Indians interred on Deer Island. Even John Pynchon, one of the most powerful men in the colony, was not free from suspicion. Residents of the town of Springfield (most of the land of which he owned) called for his death upon hearing that an Indian man who might have taken part in recent attacks was in the town. Pynchon sent him to English forces for safety, whereupon Pynchon became the target of their anger.

THE TIDE SHIFTS

But while Indian forces seemed successful, they faced growing shortages of food and declining morale. The English were getting better at coordinating efforts between their colonies, and they started employing Christian Indian scouts and (perhaps as a result) began to change their tactics: targeting Native American food stores and harassing Indian groups with small hit-and-run raids rather than seeking a major battle in the open. The Indians also had a run of bad luck. They lost one of their most effective leaders when Canonchet was captured on April 3 by Connecticut and Mohegan troops led by James Avery and George Denison. They took the Narragansett sachem to Stonington, where he was quickly executed. An attack on Bridgewater on May 8 sputtered when a huge rainstorm extinguished the fires they had set and provided an opening for the settlers to rally and drive out the warriors, inflicting many casualties.

Divisions widened between and among tribes. In early to late April, the Indians camped at Wachusett negotiated with Boston authorities, exchanging Rowlandson for a ransom and the possibility of peace. The two Christian Indians sent by officials in Boston as ambassadors reported that the Native American sachems and counselors were divided between those increasingly reluctant to pursue the war, particularly older Nipmuc sachems, and a few younger war hawks, most notably Metacom and the Narragansett Quinnapin, who rejected any negotiation. Even the Indians' victory at Sudbury was discouraging to those encamped at Mount Wachusett, as Rowlandson later wrote.

> Yet they came home [to the camp at Wachusett] without that rejoicing and triumphing over their victory, which they were wont to show at other times, but rather like dogs (as they say) which have lost their ears. Yet I could not perceive that it was for their own loss of men: they said, they had not lost above five or six: and I missed none, except in one wigwam. When they went, they acted as if the devil had told them that they should gain the victory: and now they acted, as if the devil had told them they should have a fall. Whether it were so or no, I cannot tell, but so it proved, for quickly they began to fall, and so held on that summer, till they came to utter ruin.[22]

Starvation and disease were growing problems. According to James the Printer, the literate Christian Nipmuc whom Rowlandson met at Wachusett, more warriors had died from disease than from English bullets.

The tide of the war shifted rapidly and noticeably in late May and early June 1676. By the end of April, many of the

Native Americans in the Connecticut River Valley had moved to camps at Peskeompskut, along the Connecticut River, five miles north of the abandoned town of Deerfield, to take advantage of the excellent fishing at the falls. An English captive, Thomas Reed, escaped from the camp and made it to Hatfield. There he reported to Captain William Turner, who organized a force of 150 untrained men. On May 18, Turner's forces successfully surprised the camp, slaughtering more than 100 women and children and destroying their food stores along with two forges and lead used for the Indians' weapons. Angry warriors returned to the camp too late to stop the massacre, but attacked the militia on its way home, scattering the English and then hunting down and killing 39 men, including Turner. The Indians then reorganized their forces and, seeking to renew the war and obtain their revenge, attacked Hatfield on May 30, killing seven residents, grabbing cattle, and burning many buildings.

At this point, the United Colonies decided to organize a large joint offensive, sending Captain Daniel Henchman west from Boston through Nipmuc country via Mount Wachusett, and Major John Talcott with 440 colonists and Mohegans up the Connecticut River Valley. The two forces would meet in Hadley. Along the way, the colonists surprised and captured or killed about 100 Indians. The Connecticut troops reached Hadley first, just in time to defend the town against a large attack on June 12. Legend has it that as the Pocumtucks were about to overwhelm the town, the residents were rallied by an elderly man. That man was William Goffe, a member of the English High Court of Justice who in 1649 sentenced King Charles I to death, and who in 1660 (with the restoration of Charles II to the throne) had fled to Puritan Massachusetts to hide. Unable to take Hadley, the Pocumtucks abandoned the war; most of the survivors moved north or west, out of the reach of the colonists. A force sent out of the town on June 16 to scour the valley found only abandoned Indian villages.

A member of the English High Court of Justice who signed
the death warrant for King Charles I, William Goffe fled
England for America after the monarchy was reinstated
in 1664. According to legend, Goffe rallied the citizens
of Hadley, Massachusetts, right before a large force of
Pocumtucks were about to capture the town in June 1676.

Why did the Indian uprising collapse so quickly? Most historians point to English superiority in arms and organization, which took time to adjust to the particular conflict and to become effective. The colonists also had the advantage of widely shared ethnic and religious identity and motivations, including not only survival but also a strong sense of English and Christian superiority. By comparison, the Indians had many different tribal and village allegiances, many dialects and languages, and many different reasons to fight against the English; they therefore did not share the same commitment or goals, and therefore were more willing to compromise and declare an end to the war when conditions became intolerable. Some were Christian Nipmucs who had been compelled to accompany the "hostiles" who had entered one of the praying towns at the start of the war, and were at best ambivalent about their position. Metacom's allies were aware that the dreaded Mohawks were headed their way, and that they would soon be squeezed between the two foes. Since the Mohawks generally subjected their captives to slow, agonizing torture, surrendering to the English probably seemed like a better alternative.

COLONIAL FORCES GAIN CONTROL

The English also proved willing to change tactics to turn the tide, as exemplified by Plymouth's commission to Benjamin Church. Before the war, Church had excellent relations with various Wampanoag leaders, had tried to get the colonial forces to move more quickly against Metacom to prevent his escape at the beginning of the war, and as the war progressed urged the United Colonies to make more liberal use of Indian scouts and to adopt Indian tactics. In June 1676, after a winter at home, he was given command of a small force of Wampanoag and English soldiers to hunt down the enemy. Plymouth also authorized a second force of 150 Englishmen and 50 Indians to be commanded by William Bradford, son of the first governor of the colony. Church had a particularly dramatic start: On his way home, he stumbled across Sakon-net warriors and negotiated a meeting with Awashonks. The conference was initially tense, but old friendships and shared rum and tobacco smoothed the negotiations. Awashonks of-fered to leave her alliance with Metacom and to have her men fight with his company if the tribe could retain their lands. Church and the Plymouth authorities agreed, and on June 30 the Sakonnets surrendered.

As Metacom's allies fled or began to seek peace and the force at Mount Wachusett dissolved, the colonies could begin to think of winning rather than surviving. On June 19, Mas-sachusetts officials declared that they would show "mercy" to Indians who surrendered (although, rather than clem-ency, this apparently meant a quick trial and execution, or enslavement in the Indies instead of immediate death). At the end of the month, Connecticut sent Major John Talcott's force of colonial militia and Mohegans to pursue the Nip-muc and Narragansett remnants into northern Rhode Island. Connecticut militia from the easternmost towns also made forays into Nipmuc and Narragansett territory, killing and driving many away. On July 2, Talcott attacked a large village along a swamp with few warriors; when the smoke cleared three hours later, the attackers had killed 34 men and 137 women and children (including Ninigret's sister Quaiapen), and only 45 women and children survived, probably because the Mohegans persuaded Talcott to let them live. The next day, they massacred 67 Narragansetts, including Potuck, the sachem who was waiting at Warwick to surrender. Rhode Is-land officials condemned Talcott's violation of their territory, but the damage had been done. On July 15, Ninigret signed an alliance with Massachusetts Bay.

In the meantime, Church had gone to Plymouth on July 5 to get permission for the recently surrendered Sakonnet warriors to join his company. The colony's authorities agreed. Church and Awashonks and her people celebrated the new

AWASHONKS AND THE SAKONNETS SURRENDER TO CHURCH

In the summer of 1676, the English colonists gained the initiative in the war and began hunting down the Indian forces that were scattering to seek food and refuge. Plymouth authorized Benjamin Church, who spoke fluent Wampanoag and had developed a reputation as an officer who understood Native American ways and warfare, to raise a small force of English and Indian men. As he headed home to begin recruiting soldiers, he stumbled across Sakonnet warriors on Cape Cod and negotiated a meeting with their sachem Awashonks, whom he had been friends with before the war.

June 1676

[Church] was no sooner landed, but Awashonks and the rest that he had appointed to meet him there, rose up and came down to meet him; and each of them successively gave him their hands, and expressed themselves glad to see him, and gave him thanks for exposing himself to visit them. They walked together about a Gun-shot from the water to a convenient place to sit down. Where at once a-rose up a great body of Indians, who had lain hid in the grass, (that was as high as a Mans waste) and gathered round them, till they had closed them in; being all armed with Guns, Spears, Hatchets, etc. with their hair trimmed and faces painted, in their Warlike appearance. It was doubtless some-what surprising to our Gentleman at first, but without any visible discovery of it, after a small silent pause on each side, He spoke to Awashonks, and told her, That George had informed him that she had a desire to see him, and discourse about making Peace with the English. She answered, Yes. Then said Mr. Church, It is customary when People meet to treat of Peace to lay aside their Arms, and not to appear in such Hostile form as your People do: desired of her that if they might talk about Peace, which he desired they might, Her men might

(continues)

(continued)

lay aside their Arms, and appear more treatable. Upon which there began a considerable noise and murmur among them in their own Language. Till Awashonks asked him, What Arms they should lay down, and where? He (perceiving the Indians looked very surly, and much displeased) Replied, Only their Guns at some small distance, for formality sake. Upon which with one consent they laid aside their Guns, and came and sat down.

[Church and Awashonks then shared rum and tobacco, and her counselors prevented a warrior from killing him.] . . . After some further discourse, and debate, he brought them at length to consent that if the Government of Plymouth would firmly ingage to them, That they, and all of them, and their Wives and Children, should have their Lives spared, and none of them transported out of the Country, they would subject themselve to them, and serve them in what they were able. . . . The chief Captain rose up, and expressed the great value and respect he had for Mr. Church; and bowing to him said, Sir, If you'll please to accept of me and my men, and will head us, we'll fight for you, and will help you to Philips head before Indian Corn be ripe.*

* Benjamin Church, *Entertaining Passages Relating to Philip's War* (Boston: B. Green, 1716), reprinted in *So Dreadful a Judgement: Puritan Responses to King Philip's War, 1676–1677*, Richard Slotkin and James K. Folsom, eds. (Middletown, Conn.: Wesleyan University Press, 1978), 424–426.

alliance with a grand feast along Buzzard's Bay, and by July 11 his force, with 140 Indians and 60 Englishmen, was storming through the area around Metacom's home territory. The use by Church and Bradford of Indian warriors and strategies became increasingly effective. Warriors surrendered throughout the summer, and some then agreed to fight with the English and help find their former comrades. The large party that surrendered in Cambridge on July 2 included the Christian Nipmuc James the Printer, who before the war had helped John Eliot translate the Bible into Algonquian, and during the war served as the scribe for the Narragansett and Nipmuc sachems.

The divisions among the Indians who fought the colonists became clear with the negotiations in early July between Nipmuc sachems and Boston authorities (including Waban and John Eliot). On July 6, a group of four who had been leaders in the prewar praying towns sent a message to Boston, telling the colonists that they would "make a Covenant of Peace with you . . . by *Jesus Christ.*" Soon thereafter, Sam Sachem, one of those who had signed the letter, informed Boston that, after a recent series of defeats, Metacom and Quinnapin had left Wachusett for their home territory around Narragansett Bay, since "they were much afraid, because of our offer to joyn with the *English.*" He noted that when the two war leaders heard that the English were sending delegates to offer terms for peace, "*Philip* and *Quanapun* sent [a messenger telling us] to kill them; but I said, If any kill them, I'll kill them." About the same time, several other Nipmucs sent a note pledging that if the governor's council "had sent word to Kill Philip we should have done it." In reply, the council told the Nipmucs "*That treacherous Persons who began the War, and those that have been barbarously bloody, must not expect to have their lives spared, but others that have been drawn into the War, and acting only as Souldiers submitting, to be without Arms, and to live quietly and peaceably for the future shall have their lives spared.*"[23] On July 27, the Nipmuc sachem Sagamore John surrendered in Boston, with 180 of his people and (hoping to win clemency) the bound Nipmuc sachem Matoonas, who the colonists marched to the commons and shot.

War Ended in the South and Rekindled in the North

As the summer of 1676 wore on, Plymouth's companies and the Connecticut militia continued to patrol Wampanoag territory and captured or killed the remaining Native Americans who had fled from Mount Wachusett to their homeland. The survivors still seemed to pose a danger to the colonists; on July 11, Bradford's forces (who had received warning) repelled an attack on Taunton. But the English had the clear advantage over the disheartened Indians, and during the next week the two companies killed hundreds of small groups of warriors who sought to hide in the area around Swansea, where the war began. Metacom's chief lieutenant, Nimrod, also known as Woonashum, was killed August 1, protecting his sachem's escape from a swamp 12 miles northwest of Providence. Five days later, the English captured about 25 Wampanoags and found the body of Weetamoo, the "squaw sachem" of the Pocassets and wife of the powerful Narragansett sachem Quinnapin (master of Mary Rowlandson during her captivity); it appeared she had drowned or been killed while trying to escape. The English took the body and stuck her head on a pole in the center of Taunton. Local militia also occasionally went after the fugitives. At the end of July, men from Dedham found Pomham and his Narragansett band, and killed the sachem and many of his people.

Major Talcott also continued his campaign. On July 13, he surprised and killed about 60 Indians near Pautuxet, and several days later attacked a Narragansett band, capturing 30 and killing 20, including the tribe's war sachem Pumham. As the month ended, Talcott and his troops headed west, pursuing the surviving Native Americans attempting to escape across the border into New York, where Governor Andros had declared in May that any Indians would be welcome if they maintained the peace. On August 15, the Connecticut forces hammered a sizeable group camped in the Housatonic River Valley, at present-day Great Barrington, capturing 20 and killing 35.

Most important to the English was capturing or killing Metacom, who symbolized the uprising and upon whom the English (and many Indians) placed the blame for all of the war's bloodshed and destruction. Church's force was very close to the fugitive sachem, and knew that he was in his home territory of Mount Hope. On August 1 and 3, they saw and almost killed Metacom, but they did capture his wife Wootonekanuska and his nine-year-old son—both of whom would be sold into slavery in the West Indies. A major break came on August 11, when Alderman, a Wampanoag with a grudge against Metacom for possibly ordering his brother's death, agreed to lead Church to where the sachem camped on the southwest side of Mount Hope. The next day, they surprised the camp and Alderman shot Metacom as he tried to escape. Church had the sachem's corpse dragged to shore, and then summoned "his old *Indian* executioner" who said of Metacom that *"He had been a very great man, and had made many a man afraid of him, but so big as he was, he would now chop his arse for him."*[24] The man beheaded and quartered Metacom: Church hung each quarter in a different tree and gave a hand to Alderman, who earned money by showing it around

In August 1676, the Wampanoag Alderman, whose brother had been killed by Metacom, led English forces to Metacom's camp on the southwest side of Mount Hope (near present-day Bristol, Rhode Island). As Metacom tried to escape, Alderman shot him, and Metacom was subsequently beheaded and quartered by the English.

the colonies—supposedly preserved in a bucket of rum. When Plymouth authorities heard the news, they called for a day of thanksgiving on August 17; soon after Reverend John Cotton finished his sermon, Church arrived with the sachem's head, which was paraded through the town and then put on a tall post for all to see. Decades later the head disappeared, possibly stolen by Wampanoags who buried it in a secret place.

The final act of the war in the southeast was the capture of the war chief Annawon, a Wampanoag leader since Massasoit's time. In late August, Church learned from captured Wampanoags that Annawon's band was camped in a nearby swamp.

The evening of August 28, Church's company entered the swamp at Rehoboth, Massachusetts. He decided to approach the camp from behind by descending a cliff face and then having an elderly Indian man and the man's daughter—who had told him of Annawon's location—go in front so the war leader, Church wrote later, would not notice the plot. When Church darted out and seized the stacked weapons, Attawon gave up without a fight and, seemingly impressed with Church's courage and daring, had his women prepare dinner for them to eat together. At the end of the night, Attawon went and retrieved the wampum belts that Metacom wore around his body and head, and handed them to Church telling him "in plain *English*" that *"you have killed Philip and conquered his Country, for I believe that I & my company are the last that War against the English, so suppose the War is ended by your means, and therefore these things belong to you."* In the morning, Church marched Attawon and his band to Taunton. The colonists beheaded the Wampanoag war chief a few days later. The following spring, Governor Winslow sent the belts and Metacom's other possessions to the king of England. Those items disappeared and have never been found.[25]

DEFEAT AND PUNISHMENT

Massachusetts, Connecticut, and even Rhode Island passed laws authorizing capital punishment for the surrendering Indians, because, in the eyes of the colonists, the Native Americans were traitors and war criminals. Many were quickly put to death, particularly the Native American leaders and any warriors who had been Christians or members of praying towns before the war. One of the first executed was Matoonas, the Christian Nipmuc leader of Pachacoog, who had led the assault on Mendon on July 15, 1675—almost exactly a year before he was tied to a tree in Boston commons and shot. In August, about 30 prisoners were hung from the same tree, and a month later 15 Indians were shot or hung there.

THE LOST WAR

This private account of the end of the war illuminates the political and military disasters suffered by the Indians in the summer of 1676 and their terrible personal losses from disease and hunger— but also those suffered at the hands of the English and their Native American allies. The writer, a Rhode Island magistrate, paints Connecticut forces and the Mohawks as particularly vicious and his own colony as a refuge for Native Americans seeking peace.

Ever since the taking of the great man of Narragansett [Pessicus] the war hath gone most against the Indians, and within two or three days after a great army of Indians, supposed a thousand, boasted of their victories at Providence over the English, in a parley there the afore-said great man was taken by Connecticut forces, from which time March to this 12th of August 1676, two thousand Indians have been killed taken & come in and supposed fifteen hundred before, and some say a thousand English from the first slain, but I doubt nearer fifteen hundred.

The Indians come in daily, and fight presently against the Indians they came from and betray one another into the hands of the English.

And because Connecticut forces are most constantly active & kill all save boys & girls, the Indians haste into the Massachusetts & Plymouth to [e]scape them that are most like (by the help of Indians that are with them) to kill them.

Another occasion of their coming in is want of powder, which is hard to be got now, having but little to buy it and go to buy it in great danger of their lives by reason of the Indians called Mohawks, their enemies, that meet with them that used to kill & eat their enemies but formerly they have said they had powder of the Dutch about Fort Albany.

(continues)

(continued)

There have more Indians died since the war began by sickness & hunger than by the sword, so that dead come in & transported since the war each way about seven thousand. It hath been God's heavy hand on them as well as on the English, for they now are not only in danger of the English & divers sorts of Indians but of their own supposed friends having been so much trepanned [entrapped] by them that they are afraid of all they see but least of those of Rhode Island, for there they come in & are as well accommodated as ever they were in their lives only they are called servants, but soon after peace is concluded they will run all away again as the captives formerly did after the Pequot War forty years since . . .

Just now news is brought that this 12th of August early in the morning Philip was slain in a swamp within a mile of Mount Hope [his home] & about a mile & half from Rhode Island. He was with a few men there & set upon by one Captain Benjamin Church of Plymouth & Captain Pealeg Sanford of Rhode Island, each of them with forty men, & they said Philip was shot through the heart by an Indian that lives on Rhode Island and his head & hands are now on the said Island.*

---

* William Harris, *Papers, Rhode Island Historical Society Collections 10* (Providence, 1902), 177–78, reprinted in *Puritans, Indians, and Manifest Destiny*, Charles M. Segal and David C. Stineback, eds. (New York: G. P. Putnam's Sons, 1977), 199–200.

Also hung there were several prominent Christian Indians from Hassanamisset, most notably Peter Jethro and his father "Old Jethro," who had gone along with raiding Nipmucs at the beginning of the war.

The victorious and vindictive colonial authorities even felt free to ignore pardons given by their commanders. The Nipmuc sachems Muttawmp and Sagamore John (Shoshonin), who had led successful attacks and devastated colonial forces at New Braintree, Brookfield, Bloody Brook, and Sudbury, were given amnesty by Richard Waldron in exchange for bringing in Monoco, who accepted a similar offer from Waldron. Massachusetts authorities executed all three in Boston in September 1676. That same month, Metacom's brother-in-law Tispaquin surrendered to Benjamin Church after getting assurances that he and his men would be given amnesty and enlisted to fight with the English in Maine—but the "Black Sachem" was immediately shot by Plymouth authorities. Similarly, on August 25, the Narragansett sachem Quinnapin (Weetamoo's husband) was shot at Newport even though he had been given quarter when he surrendered. The Narragansett sachem Potuck had, in early July, gone to Rhode Island seeking to surrender and was granted safe conduct and clemency to go to Newport to negotiate terms. Instead, Massachusetts authorities executed him as a war criminal.

Most of those not executed were sold into slavery. The Puritan ministers and magistrates debated whether this was a humane policy, but decided that it was a better alternative than putting to death all of those who had opposed the United Colonies. Doing the same to the warriors' women and children was also seen as justifiable according to the Bible, and useful in obtaining African slaves to work in the New England colonies. The governors of Massachusetts and Plymouth justified this enslavement by pointing to Metacom's betrayal of his treaties with the colonists and his resulting treason against the king's sovereignty. Indian captives sold for about three pounds per person, which proved a lucrative source of income for the colonies and individual merchants. Some Native Americans were purchased by colonists for domestic or farm laborers, but most (about 1,000) were transported to Jamaica and Barbados in the West Indies. The market was so profitable that some colonists had their Indian slaves stolen by thieves who sold them elsewhere. Probably most of them quickly died on the sugar plantations, although some passed their stories to children, who passed their memories to their descendants.

WAR RENEWED IN THE NORTH

While the war sputtered to an end in southern New England, many Pennacook, Nipmuc, and Narragansett warriors who had fled the war in the south went north and found refuge among the Wabanakis. The stories and anger that they carried with them seem to have spurred the renewal of war against the colonists. On August 11, one day before Metacom's death, Squando's Saco warriors attacked Falmouth, killing or capturing 34 English and causing the colonists to abandon the town. Two days later, the Wabanakis attacked a trading post, killing its owner Richard Hammond and taking many others captive. The warriors divided into two groups, one of which traveled to Arrowsic, where the next day they seized and destroyed another trading post, owned by Thomas Clarke and Thomas Lakes. The colonists at Pemaquid, fearing attack, burned and abandoned their own town. Like many others, they headed for Salem, Massachusetts, where many had relatives and others could find refuge. By the end of the month, the English had abandoned the region northeast of Scarborough, Maine.

Massachusetts sent a large force to Richard Waldron in southern New Hampshire in order to reinforce the settlements in southern Maine and pursue the enemy. The colonial forces included Wampanoag and Massachusett units commanded by Benjamin Church. Waldron pursued a scorched-earth strategy that gave no quarter, looked to gain no allies, and rarely distinguished between friend and foe. One incident became particularly notorious. On September 7, 1676, Waldron invited about 400 Wabanakis to a peace conference at his home at Quechecho, hoping that some of the Nipmucs and Narragansetts would also come. Waldron offered the Indians barrels of rum to celebrate the peace, but when they became drunk his men seized around 200 "that had been our Enemies" and sent them to Boston where they were executed or enslaved. Waldron's deceptions and his savage strategies

After Metacom's death, Major Richard Waldron led a campaign to track down and kill any surviving Nipmucs and Narragansetts (and any other tribe he encountered). On September 7, 1676, he invited 400 Wabanakis to a peace conference at his home in Quechecho (in present-day southern New Hampshire) but captured half of them and sold them into slavery. Thirteen years later, Waldron had his comeuppance when he was tortured and killed at the hands of the Wabanakis (depicted here).

would lead to his agonizing death by torture at the hands of Wabanaki attackers 13 years later.

The Wabanakis continued their attacks, and English efforts to stop them were notably unsuccessful. In October, the Kennebec sachem Mugg Hegone won the surrender of the fort at Black Point, near Scarborough, without firing a shot. The Wabanakis had driven nearly all of the English from their territory. Hegone and his Penobscot ally Madockawando hoped to use the victory to obtain a favorable peace agreement with Massachusetts, and in November sent a mission to Boston to negotiate. But the colonial authorities insisted on very strict terms, including reparations for damages done to settler property and the return of all English captives, many of whom were held by groups over which the two sachems had no authority.

Wabanaki trust dipped lower in February, when, at a conference with Penobscot sachems to discuss peace, Waldron again used deception to disarm and seize the Indian leaders. These events sent many Indian refugees deep into the interior, settling at Schaghticoke and St. Francis (Odanak) in Quebec, and ensured that the war would continue as a series of small-scale raids against English settlements. In April, Simon "the Yankee Killer" raided York and Wells, killing 10. In May, Hegone and his warriors besieged the new garrison at Black Point, although this time the attackers would find the defenses too difficult, and their sachem was among those killed. The warriors withdrew and doubled back to hit York and Wells again, killing seven residents. That summer, the Wabanakis successfully stole 20 English fishing boats from Salem that were anchored in Maine waters; the raiders stripped and abandoned the ships. English raids against Indian villages, on the other hand, found only empty villages, as their inhabitants retreated to the interior.

As with the war in the south, the Mohawks and the New York governor got involved. In June 1677, New York governor Edmund Andros took control of Pemaquid Fort and the surrounding Sagadahoc Province in Maine. That spring, Massachusetts delegates obtained a promise by the Mohawks to enter the war. Perhaps as a result of the Mohawk threat and New York's soothing presence, in July the Kennebecs asked Massachusetts Bay Colony authorities for a truce and treaty. They were met with a bland promise that the abuses of the past would be solved by more orderly English settlement in the future. Since the Bay Colony's terms were vague and unacceptable, the Wabanakis turned to Sagadahoc, whose commanders brokered a truce in August 1677, formalized in the Casco Treaty of April 1678. As an uneasy peace settled over the region, many Wabanakis began returning to their homes in a pattern that would become common as subsequent wars rocked the region.

The Results and Memories of King Philip's War

KING PHILIP'S WAR WAS THE BLOODIEST WAR IN American history in terms of its proportionate effect on New England. Of the approximately 80,000 people living in the region in May 1675, nearly 9,000 (more than 10 percent) were killed; a third of the casualties were English and two-thirds were Indians. The political and cultural effects on the people in the region were equally significant and longer lasting, creating a scarred memory that still rankled 150 years later.

The consequences for Native Americans were particularly severe, as their numbers in southern New England decreased by about half, from 25 percent to only about 10 percent of the population in the region. About 3,000 died from combat, disease, or hunger; about 2,000 refugees left the region, mostly for the Hudson River Valley; and about 1,000 were sold into slavery and certain death in the West Indies. In 1698, six years after Plymouth was annexed to Massachusetts, that colony counted 4,168 Indians. The war also meant the end of Indian sovereignty east of the Connecticut River. While there remained in the area about 25 communities with territories (of various sizes) reserved for their use and residence, only the Narragansetts and Mohegans retained a substantive level of autonomy, retaining their sachems and councils without the direct oversight of guardians appointed by the provincial legislature.

Also badly mauled were the New England colonists, particularly in Massachusetts. Thousands lost their relatives and became refugees. Of 90 towns in New England, 52 (58 percent) were attacked, 25 pillaged (more than one-fourth), and 17 razed. Nearly all of the towns in Massachusetts more than 20 miles west of Boston were abandoned. All but a few of those in Nipmuc territory were not resettled until after the Treaty of Utrecht between France and England in 1713 ended the potential of attack by Wabanakis and their allies. While the coalition led by Massachusetts won the war in the south, that colony in the wake of its victory (ironically) also lost much of its sovereignty. In June 1676, Boston authorities were confronted by Edward Randolph when he returned to America as a royal commissioner sent to bring the Massachusetts Bay Colony to heel. His arrival began a political struggle there and in London over who would control the province, which saw a continuation of the wartime conflicts. In 1682, the Crown formally challenged the Massachusetts charter in proceedings in which colony officials were tasked to provide evidence proving what right they had to sovereignty. This encouraged dissidents both within and outside the colony. Four years later, the colony lost its charter and was folded into the Dominion of New England. While Massachusetts would regain some autonomy with the Revolution of 1688 in England and a new charter in 1692, it would never be able to claim the sovereignty it held before the war.

INDIAN ALLIES IN THE WAKE OF THE WAR

Although they allowed some Native American groups to resettle their villages and farm their lands, the colonists shared few of the spoils with their Indian allies. In May 1678, the

Mohegans, led by Uncas and his son Oweneco, reconfirmed their loyalty to the English, but received little for their assistance other than new tribe members—individual Indians who had surrendered to the Mohegans rather than the English. Connecticut demanded that every captive taken by their allies be identified and limited to reservations, supervised by English rulers and teachers, and that the younger Indians be placed as servants with English families for 10 years. Massachusetts and Rhode Island also placed with English families the captive Indian children who were not sold to the West Indies, providing a source of needed labor as well as social control over potentially disruptive individuals. Many River Indians, such as the Sakonnets, Pequots, and Niantics, including some individuals who had fought against the English, were allowed to resettle their communities under colonial protection.

The Christian Indians who survived internment on the Boston islands were released in May 1676. But provincial officials did not allow the former praying Indians to return to their towns, instead placing the survivors under the oversight of white guardians near Boston. The Indians divided into two groups: Those who had lived at Natick or the Nipmuc towns, led by Waban, went first to Cambridge and then to Nonantum (Waban's village in the 1640s); the Punkapoags (mostly Massachusett) settled at Brush Hill near Milton. In the spring of 1677, the Punkapoags returned to their village and Waban's people fanned out to Natick and a few other praying towns to plant their crops and work as farm laborers for the English. But many who tried to resettle to their praying towns met bitter opposition from colonists who had seized their personal belongings and real estate.

In addition, continuing Mohawk raids initially forced the Indians to retreat to English population centers. In April 1677, Massachusetts and Connecticut sent representatives to Albany to negotiate for the continued pursuit of enemy forces in Maine, and an end to attacks on friendly Indians living along the Connecticut River. News of an agreement provided sufficient encouragement for the Indians to resettle Natick and Punkapoag in September 1677. But raiding parties continued to make the edges of English settlement very hazardous, and indeed the two resettled praying towns built forts against future attacks. That fall Mohawks captured two elderly women when they went to Hassanamisset to make cider, and less than a year later warriors carried off 22 Natick Indians from cornfields in the adjoining praying town of Magunkaquog; such captives were usually adopted or tortured to death. That summer, Massachusetts delegates returned to Albany to negotiate for the safe return of their allies, with limited success; two years later, Connecticut gave the Mohegans permission to assist the Naticks against the Mohawks. But the raids continued. In July 1680, a group of Massachuset Indians living at Spy Pond in Cambridge— only a few miles from where the General Court met—were attacked by Mohawks; two were killed and several others carried away.

Despite such problems, these Christian Indian groups managed to increase their autonomy, particularly after John Eliot died in 1690, and provincial laws barred the sale of their lands without permission of the assembly. A decade later, when Massachusetts annexed New Plymouth, Indian praying towns there obtained similar protections. But throughout the eighteenth century, these remaining communities were battered by changes in the colonial economy, by the terrible effects of epidemics, alcoholism, and indebtedness, and by the loss of men in wars or to migratory labor. The survivors adapted by teetering along the line between isolation from and immersion in colonial society and culture, seeking to satisfy their needs in the new environment while maintaining critical boundaries against white settlers. By the American Revolution, only a handful of Indian towns remained, largely acculturated to English ways and led by Native American ministers who preached in the Wampanoag language.

THE MEMORY OF THE WAR

New England ministers and magistrates began arguing over the meaning and memory of the war even before it ended. In December 1675, Nathaniel Saltonstall published in London *The Present State of New-England with Respect to the Indian War*, which presented a sparse list of the terrible events; the following February John Easton's *Relacion of the Indyan War* presented his meeting with Metacom and a Quaker view of the causes of the war. In May, even before Metacom's death, Increase Mather, the minister of North Church in Boston and the colony's intellectual and political leader, began writing a history to depict the war in properly Calvinist terms: as punishment for the colonists' sins, including men wearing their hair long, the colonists' greed, and not doing enough to convert the Indians. Mather's *A Brief History of the Warr with the Indians in New-England* would be the first fairly complete account of the war, published in fall 1676 in Boston and London.

The following spring, William Hubbard, the minister at Ipswich and Mather's competitor, published a very different *Narrative of the Troubles with the Indians in New-England*. This work depicted essentialist differences between the Native Americans and the English in moral and racial terms, accusing all Indians of savage "Malice" regardless of their religion. The other significant contemporary depiction of the war, Mary Rowlandson's *The Sovereignty and Goodness of God* (1682), presented a view of the Christian and the enemy Indians that was closer to Hubbard's account than Mather's. Her work would serve as the prototype for thousands of eighteenth- and nineteenth-century American captivity narratives.

Despite their disagreements about the causes and nature of the war, all these authors shared one characteristic: they were

A

BRIEF HISTORY

OF THE

VVARR

With the *INDIANS* in

NEVV-ENGLAND,

(From *June 24, 1675.* when the first English-man was murdered by the Indians, to *August 12. 1676.* when *Philip, alias
Metacomet,* the principal Author and Beginner
of the Warr, was slain.)
Wherein the Grounds, Beginning, and Progress of the Warr,
is summarily expressed.

TOGETHER WITH A SERIOUS

EXHORTATION

to the Inhabitants of that Land,

By *INCREASE MATHER,* Teacher of a Church of
Christ, in *Boston* in *New-England.*

Levit. 26 25. *I will bring a Sword upon you, that shall avenge the quarrel of the Co-
venant.*
Psal. 107 43. *Whoso is wise and will observe these things, even they shall understand the
Loving-kindness of the Lord*
Jer. 22.15. *Did not thy Father doe Judgment and Justice, and it was well with him?*

Segnius irritant animos demissa per aures,
Quàm quæ sunt oculis commissa fidelibus.   *Horat.*
Lege Historiam ne fias Historia.   *Cic.*

BOSTON,   Printed and Sold by *John Foster* over
against the Sign of the *Dove.* 1676.

Published in the fall of 1676, Increase Mather's *A Brief
History of the Warr with the Indians in New-England* was
the first account of King Philip's War. Although Mather
believed that God was punishing the English colonists for
their neglect of religion, he argued that the colonists were
fighting a defensive war against a treacherous enemy who
had not been provoked.

English. Neither the Indians who fought the English nor those who fought for the colonists left any writings about the war to explain their reasons or experiences. Rowlandson's book and other narratives of the war would be republished in the 1770s, as New Englanders looked to their past to better understand the current threat from the British "savages" threatening their lands and liberties.

In the 1820s, a clear shift occurred in how Metacom, the war, and New England's colonial past were viewed, driven by the blossoming of literature that often included the romantic image of the Noble Indian that became an archetype with James Fenimore Cooper's *The Last of the Mohicans* (1826). The change began with Washington Irving's "Philip of Pokanoket," published in the *Analectic Magazine* in 1814, and then in his *Sketchbook* collection five years later, which recast Metacom as "a true born prince, gallantly fighting . . . to deliver his native land from the oppression of usurping strangers."[26] Others clearly felt the same way. In 1820, *Yamoyden: A Tale of the War of King Philip*, an ode by James Eastburn and Robert Charles Sands, cast the Native Americans as suffering "foul oppressions" from the Puritans who reeked of "soulless bigotry" and "avarice."[27]

A decade later, the already-famous American actor Edwin Forrest commissioned a play featuring a Native American hero. *Metamora, Or the Last of the Wampanoags*, became a hit throughout the United States as Forrest took the play to every major city during the following two decades. Audiences wept as Philip's wife and child were captured by hostile Puritans, and at the conclusion of the play "rose in wild and reportedly 'rapturous' applause" when the mortally wounded sachem cried "curses on you, white men! . . . The last of the Wampanoags' curse be on you!"[28] Ironically, many delegations of western Indian tribes visiting American cities in the 1830s and 1840s were taken to see the play. Many of the children's books published for the growing state education systems, which began in Massachusetts in the mid-1830s, similarly extolled Metacom as a selfless and heroic defender of his people and their land, and some condemned the Puritan colonists. Samuel Goodrich's *Lives of Celebrated American Indians: by the Author of Peter Parley's Tales* (Boston, 1843) called the Wampanoag leader "a savage indeed, and a ruthless enemy, yet a patriot and statesman."

The story of Metacom's ill-treatment and his resistance was also used by New Englanders to condemn the emerging U.S. Indian policy of forcing the Cherokee and other tribes (mostly in the southeastern United States) to remove west of the Mississippi River. Several reformers wrote novels celebrating the Wampanoag sachem, including Sarah Savage who, in *Life of Philip* (1827), called him "a penetrating statesman, a great warrior, a noble, disinterested, self-denying patriot."[29] In 1833, the Pequot Methodist minister William Apess led the Mashpee revolt for more autonomy in Massachusetts and justified their armed resistance in terms of the state's support of the Cherokees' political resistance to removal. Three years later, he was applauded by Boston's elite at the city's Odeon Theater as he compared Metacom to George Washington and called the Wampanoag sachem "the greatest man that was ever in America."[30]

But this sympathy for Metacom and Indian resistance did not mean that New Englanders were ready to make restitution and restore sovereignty or land to Indian descendants still living in the region. Instead, King Philip's War became celebrated as part of the past that had forged a unique New England identity; the defeat of the Wampanoags and their allies was viewed as inevitable and necessary; and the survivors and their descendants were ignored or depicted as a vanished people. In August 1876, in a special celebration of the two hundredth anniversary of Metacom's death, Rhode Island's governor described the sachem's resistance as normal and expected ("Hadn't he a right to fight? Would any of us have had him do differently?"), but inevitably doomed to fail "and of course we thank God that he did." The governor also added, as so many others noted in similar anniversary celebrations, that the few remaining Indians in the region were already or would soon be extinct.[31]

Yet there were still noticeable Indian families and communities in southern New England, and they would make their own use of the memory of King Philip's War. In the audience listening to the Rhode Island governor were Melinda and Charlotte Mitchell, the daughters of Zervia Gould Mitchell. The two sisters had become celebrities as lineal descendants of Massasoit and were using this fame to press their claim to lands in the area and to sell baskets and other crafts to those attending the festival. Delegations from the Narragansett, Mohegan, Pequot, and other tribes were similarly invited to public commemorations of the war and celebrations of other important anniversaries, such as the founding of towns at or near tribal centers; they inevitably used these appearances to wear Indian dress and publicly confirm that their people and community still existed. After 1925, these Indian descendants would seek to revive their tribal cultures and memories, and in the 1970s began to push for federal recognition—which meant more autonomy and the return of tribal territories. Today, the sites and stories of King Philip's War—from Deer Island in Boston Harbor, where the Christian Indians were interred, to the Great Swamp Fight Monument in Rhode Island—have become places and opportunities for Native American peoples in southern New England to reclaim history and power.

Chronology

1621 *SEPTEMBER 21* Wampanoags and English negotiate treaty at Plymouth.

1630 English land at Shawmut Peninsula, renamed Boston; establish Massachusetts Bay Colony.

1637 *APRIL 23* Pequots attack Wethersford, beginning war.

MAY 26 English, Narragansetts, and Mohegans attack and destroy the Pequot fort at Mystic.

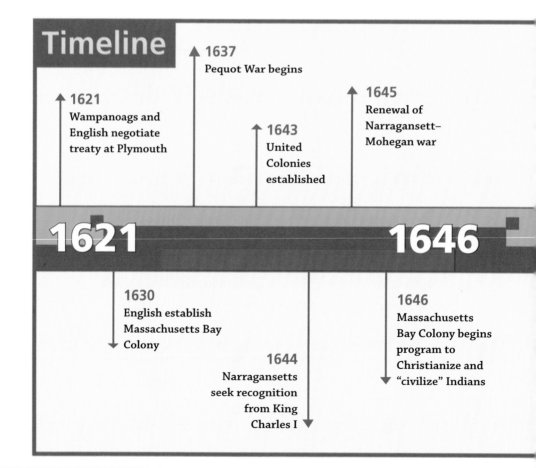

Timeline

1637
Pequot War begins

1621
Wampanoags and English negotiate treaty at Plymouth

1645
Renewal of Narragansett–Mohegan war

1643
United Colonies established

1621   **1646**

1630
English establish Massachusetts Bay Colony

1646
Massachusetts Bay Colony begins program to Christianize and "civilize" Indians

1644
Narragansetts seek recognition from King Charles I

1642 *SUMMER* Massachusetts Bay Colony suspects Narragansetts of planning pan-tribal uprising.

1643 *MAY 19* United Colonies established.

AUGUST 6 Narragansett sachem Miantonomo captured by Uncas in battle.

SEPTEMBER 7 Miantonomo brought before commissioners of the United Colonies, condemned, given to Uncas for execution.

1644 *APRIL 19* Narragansetts seek recognition from King Charles I of England.

1645 *MAY* Renewal of Narragansett–Mohegan war.

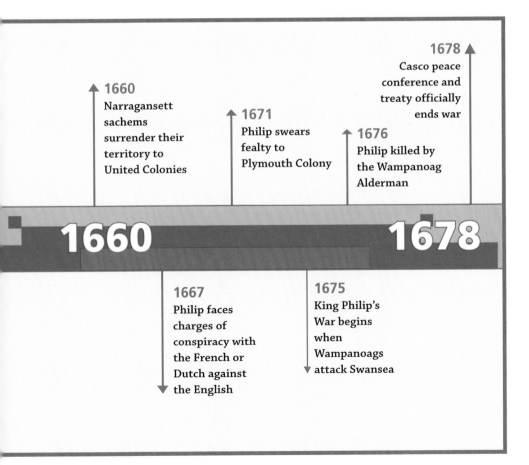

1660 Narragansett sachems surrender their territory to United Colonies

1671 Philip swears fealty to Plymouth Colony

1676 Philip killed by the Wampanoag Alderman

1678 Casco peace conference and treaty officially ends war

1660 **1678**

1667 Philip faces charges of conspiracy with the French or Dutch against the English

1675 King Philip's War begins when Wampanoags attack Swansea

AUGUST 19   United Colonies forces sent against Narragansetts, war averted at last minute.

1646   *OCTOBER 28*   Reverend John Eliot preaches for the first time at Nonantum (modern-day Newton/Watertown area), beginning the Massachusetts Bay Colony's program to Christianize and "civilize" Indians in the region.

1646–1660   "Cold war" between English and Narragansetts and their allies.

1660   *SEPTEMBER 29*   Unable to pay tribute demand in wampum, Narragansett sachems sign mortgage for all of their territory to United Colonies.

1662   *MARCH 4*   Plymouth issues order to Wamsutta (Alexander) to sell Wampanoag territory only to Plymouth.

JULY   Wamsutta arrested, becomes sick, and dies en route to Plymouth.

AUGUST 6   Plymouth sends for Metacom (Philip) to answer suspicions of plotting an uprising, to renew peace agreements, and to sell lands only with their consent.

1663   *NOVEMBER 26*   Narragansetts renew their "submission" to the king of England (now Charles II) in order to protect their land and sovereignty against the English colonists.

1667   *JULY 2*   Plymouth brings Philip to answer charges of conspiracy with the French or Dutch against the English, finding out that Ninigret invented the charges.

1671   *APRIL 10*   Plymouth forces Philip to come to Taunton; he confesses his "Unfaithfulness and Folly" and swears fealty to the colony (thereby apparently placing himself under Plymouth's rule), and as security surrenders his people's firearms.

JUNE–SEPTEMBER Sachems around Plymouth swear fealty to the colony.

SEPTEMBER 29 Plymouth summons Philip to answer charges that he was violating the April agreement.

1674 *SEPTEMBER* John Eliot and Massachusetts Indian superintendent Daniel Gookin install Christian constables and teachers at Nipmuc villages deep in the tribe's territory.

1675 *JANUARY 29* John Sassamon dies at Assawompsett Pond.

JUNE 8 Philip's three counselors executed at Plymouth for murder of Sassamon.

CA. JUNE 17 Philip meets with John Easton, deputy governor of Rhode Island.

JUNE 24 Wampanoags attack Swansea; English delegates check with Nipmucs and Narragansetts regarding their loyalty.

JUNE 26–29 Wampanoags attack Rehoboth and Taunton, get around colonial troops and evacuate Mount Hope, and cross the bay to Pocasset.

JULY 8–9 Wampanoags attack Middleborough and Dartmouth.

JULY 14 Nipmucs attack Mendon, opening a new front in the war.

JULY 15 Narragansetts sign a peace treaty with the colonies of Connecticut and Massachusetts.

JULY 16–24 Massachusetts Bay Colony envoys negotiate with Nipmucs.

JULY 29 Wampanoags attack Dartmouth, allowing Philip and his warriors to escape the English trap and head for Nipmuc territory.

AUGUST 2–4 Nipmucs attack Massachusetts troops and besiege Brookfield.

AUGUST 5   Wampanoags join forces with Nipmucs.

AUGUST 13   Massachusetts confines Christian Indians to praying towns.

AUGUST 25   After Hatfield settlers demand their weapons, Pocumtucks flee their village and, when pursued, turn and attack; another front opened in the war.

SEPTEMBER 1–2   Wampanoags and Nipmucs attack Deerfield and Squakeag.

SEPTEMBER 5   Wabanakis attack trading post on the Pejebscot River; war starts in Maine.

SEPTEMBER 12   English abandon Deerfield, Squakeag, and Brookfield.

SEPTEMBER 12–18   Wabanakis attack English outposts and settlements along Saco River.

SEPTEMBER 18   Narragansetts sign treaty with United Colonies in Boston; Battle of Bloody Brook, south of Deerfield.

OCTOBER 5   Pocumtucks attack Springfield; repulsed after doing little damage.

OCTOBER 30   Massachusetts confines Christian Indians to Deer Island; Wabanakis attack Wells, York, and other towns and settlements in Maine.

NOVEMBER 1   Nipmucs take Christian Indians from Hassanamisset and other villages.

DECEMBER 19   In the "Great Swamp Fight," United Colonies forces attack Narragansetts.

1676   Philip travels to Mohawk territory to seek an alliance, but is attacked and retreats.

JANUARY 27   Narragansetts emerge from hiding; attack Pawtuxet and head to join Nipmucs and Wampanoags at Mount Wachusett.

FEBRUARY 10 Nipmucs and others attack Lancaster; Mary Rowlandson taken captive.

FEBRUARY 21 Nipmucs and Narragansetts attack Medfield, Massachusetts.

MARCH 2, 9, AND 13 Nipmucs attack Groton, Massachusetts.

MARCH 12 Wampanoags attack Clark home near Plymouth.

MARCH 14 Pocumtucks and allies attack Northampton, Massachusetts.

MARCH 16 Warwick, Rhode Island, attacked and burned.

MARCH 26 Longmeadow, Marlborough, and Simsbury in Massachusetts attacked.

MARCH 28 Narragansetts attack Rehoboth after destroying Plymouth militia company.

MARCH 29 Narragansetts attack and destroy Providence, Rhode Island.

APRIL 3 Narragansett war sachem Canonchet captured, executed.

APRIL 9 Bridgewater and Plymouth attacked.

APRIL 17 Marlborough, Massachusetts, attacked and burned.

APRIL 21 Nipmucs and others attack Sudbury, Massachusetts; daylong battle ensues.

MAY 2–3 Mary Rowlandson released.

MAY 8–20 Wampanoags attack and burn Bridgewater, Halifax, and Scituate.

MAY 18 Colonial militia attacks Pocumtuck fishing camp, killing more than 100.

MAY 30 Pocumtucks attack Hatfield, Massachusetts.

JUNE 12 Pocumtucks attack Hadley, Massachusetts, repulsed by Connecticut soldiers.

JUNE 30   Awashonks and her Sakonnets surrender to Benjamin Church.

JULY 2   Connecticut and Mohegan forces attack Narragansett village in Rhode Island; James Printer and many other Nipmucs surrender in Cambridge.

JULY 4   Captain Benjamin Church forces sweep through Plymouth for refugees.

JULY 27   Nearly 200 Nipmucs surrender in Boston.

AUGUST 1   Metacom's chief lieutenant killed; Philip's wife and son captured.

AUGUST 11   Wabanakis attack Falmouth, Maine.

AUGUST 12   Philip killed by Alderman.

AUGUST 28   Wampanoag war leader Annawon captured by Benjamin Church.

SEPTEMBER 7   Richard Waldron invites Wabanakis to peace conference at Quechecho, seizes about 200 hundred "enemies" who are executed or enslaved.

OCTOBER 12   Mugg Hegone forces surrender of fort at Black Point near Scarborough, Maine; Wabanakis had driven nearly all of the English from their territory.

NOVEMBER   Boston peace conference falls apart.

1677   *FEBRUARY 26–27*   Richard Waldron deceives Wabanakis by calling peace conference and then seizing sachems.

APRIL–MAY   Wabanaki raids continue against English settlements and outposts.

1678   *APRIL 12*   Casco peace conference and treaty officially ends war.

Notes

Chapter 1

1. Phineas Pratt, "A Declaration of the Affairs of the English People that First Inhabited New England" (1662), in *Puritans, Indians, and Manifest Destiny*, Charles M. Segal and David C. Stineback, eds. (New York: G.P. Putnam's Sons, 1977), 60–61.

Chapter 2

2. Nathaniel Morton, "New England's Memoriall" (1669), in *Chronicles of the Pilgrim Fathers*, ed. John Masefield (New York: E.P. Dutton, 1936), 127–128.
3. John Underhill, *Nevvs from America; Or, a New and Experimentall Discoverie of New England* (1638; repr., New York: Da Capo Press, 1971), 42–43.
4. Ibid., 44.
5. John Winthrop, *Winthrop Papers* (Boston: Massachusetts Historical Society, 1929), 488–490.

Chapter 3

6. Lion Gardiner, "Lieft Lion Gardener His Relation of the Pequot Warres" (1637), *Massachusetts Historical Society Collections* 3, no. 3 (1833): 153–154.
7. John Winthrop, *The Journal of John Winthrop, 1630–1649*, Richard S. Dunn, James Savage, and Laetitia Yeandle, eds. (Cambridge Mass.: Harvard University Press, 1996), 408–412.
8. Samuel Gorton, *Samuel Gorton's Letter to Lord Hyde In Behalf of the Narragansett Sachems* (Providence, R.I.: Society of Colonial Wars, 1930); italics in original.
9. Pessicus and Canonicus to Massachusetts, 24 May 1644, *Colonial Collections* 33, no. 2, Massachusetts Archives, Boston.
10. Nathaniel B. Shurtleff, ed., *Records of the Colony of New Plymouth, in New England* 10 (Boston: W. White, 1855–61), 158.

Chapter 4

11. Shurtleff, *Records of the Colony of New Plymouth, in New England* 5, 77–80
12. Benjamin Church, "Entertaining Passages Relating to Philip's War," in *So Dreadfull A Judgment: Puritan Responses to King Philip's War, 1676–1677*, Richard Slotkin and James K. Folsom, eds. (Middletown, Conn.: Wesleyan University Press, 1978), 398–399.

Chapter 5

13. Mary Rowlandson, "The Sovereignty and Goodness of God, Together with the

Faithfulness of His Promises Displayed; Being a Narrative of the Captivity and Restoration of Mrs. Mary Rowlandson," in *So Dreadfull A Judgment*, 358.

14. Quoted in Jill Lepore, *The Name of War: King Philip's War and the Origins of American Identity* (New York: Knopf, 1998), 94, and details 283 ftnt 96.

Chapter 7

15. *Public Records of the Colony of Connecticut*, Vol. 2, 364.
16. Daniel Gookin, "An Historical Account of the Doings and Sufferings of the Christian Indians in New England, In the Years 1675, 1676, 1677," American Antiquarian Society *Transactions and Collections* 20 (1836), 485.
17. Quoted in Lepore, *The Name of War*, 92.
18. Increase Mather, *A Brief History of the War with the Indians in New England* (Boston: John Foster, 1676), in *So Dreadful a Judgment*, 112–13.

Chapter 8

19. Roger Williams, *The Correspondence of Roger Williams*, Glenn W. LaFantasie, ed. 2 vols. (Hanover, N.H.: University Press of New England, 1988), 721–24.
20. Ibid.
21. Rowlandson, in *So Dreadfull A Judgment*, 358–59.
22. Ibid., 354.

23. Anonymous, *A True Account of the Most Considerable Occurrences that Have Happened in the Warre Between the English and Indians in New-England* (London: Benjamin Billingsley, 1676), 6–7.

Chapter 9

24. Church, in *So Dreadfull A Judgment*, 451 (italics in original).
25. Ibid., 460 (italics in original).

Chapter 10

26. Washington Irving, "Philip of Pokanoket," in *The Sketch Book of Geoffrey Crayon, Gent*, (1819–20), vol. 8 in *The Complete Works of Washington Irving*, Haskell Springer, ed. (Boston: Twayne Publishers, 1978), 235.
27. Quoted in John Gorham Palfrey, "Review of *Yamoyden*," *North American Review* 12 (1820), 485.
28. Lepore, *Name of War*, 191–92.
29. Sarah Savage, *Life of Philip, the Indian Chief* (Salem, Mass.: Whipple and Lawrence, 1827), 51.
30. William Apess, "Eulogy on King Philip" (Boston, 1836), reprinted in *On Our Own Ground: The Complete Writings of William Apess, a Pequot*, Barry O'Connell, ed. (Amherst: University of Massachusetts Press, 1992), 277, 308 (quotation).
31. Lepore, *Name of War*, 234.

Bibliography

Apess, William. "Eulogy on King Philip." Boston, 1836. Reprinted in *On Our Own Ground: The Complete Writings of William Apess, a Pequot*, edited by Barry O'Connell, 275–310. Amherst: University of Massachusetts Press, 1992.

Connecticut. *Public Records of the Colony of Connecticut* (Hartford), vol. 2.

Drake, James D. *King Philip's War: Civil War in New England, 1675–1676*. Amherst: University of Massachusetts Press, 1999.

Easton, John. "A Relacion of the Indyan Warre." Albany, N.Y.: Franklin B. Hough, 1858. Reprinted in *Narratives of the Indian Wars, 1675–1699*, edited by Charles H. Lincoln, 7–17. New York: Barnes and Noble, 1913.

Gookin, Daniel. "An Historical Account of the Doings and Sufferings of the Christian Indians in New England, In the Years 1675, 1676, 1677." American Antiquarian Society *Transactions and Collections* 20 (1836): 433–534.

Irving, Washington. "Philip of Pokanoket." In *The Sketch Book of Geoffrey Crayon, Gent*. Washington Irving, Works, edited by Haskell Springer, 8. Boston: Twayne Publishers, 1978.

Leach, Douglas. *Flintlock and Tomahawk: New England in King Philip's War*. New York, Norton, 1958.

Lepore, Jill. *The Name of War: King Philip's War and the Origins of American Identity*. Boston: Knopf, 1998.

Mandell, Daniel. *Behind the Frontier: Indians in Eighteenth-century Eastern Massachusetts*. Lincoln: University of Nebraska Press, 1996.

———, ed. *Northern and Western New England Treaties*. Early American Indian Documents: Treaties and Laws, 1607–1789, Vol. 20. Baltimore, Md.: University Publications of America, 2003.

———, ed. *Southern New England Treaties*. Early American Indian Documents: Treaties and Laws, 1607–1789, Vol. 19. Baltimore, Md.: University Publications of America, 2003.

————. *Tribe, Race, History: Indians in Southern New England, 1780–1880.* Baltimore, Md.: Johns Hopkins University Press, forthcoming.

Pulsipher, Jenny Hale. *Subjects unto the Same King: Indians, English, and the Contest for Authority in Colonial New England.* Philadelphia: University of Pennsylvania Press, 2005.

Saltonstall, Nathaniel. *A New and Further Narrative of the State of New England.* London: J.B., 1676.

Savage, Sarah. *Life of Philip, the Indian Chief.* Salem, Mass.: Whipple and Lawrence, 1827.

Schultz, Eric B., and Michael Tougias. *King Philip's War: The History and Legacy of America's Forgotten Conflict.* Woodstock, Vt.: Countryman Press, 1999.

Slotkin, Richard, and James K. Folsom, eds. *So Dreadful a Judgement: Puritan Responses to King Philip's War, 1676–1677.* Middletown, Conn.: Wesleyan University Press, 1978.

Further Reading

Bourne, Russell. *The Red King's Rebellion: Racial Politics in New England, 1675–1678*. New York: Atheneum, 1990.

Jennings, Francis. *The Invasion of America: Indians, Colonialism, and the Cant of Conquest*. Chapel Hill: University of North Carolina Press, 1975.

Leach, Douglas. *Flintlock and Tomahawk: New England in King Philip's War*. New York, Norton, 1958.

Lepore, Jill. *The Name of War: King Philip's War and the Origins of American Identity*. Boston: Knopf, 1998.

Rowlandson, Mary. *The Sovereignty and Goodness of God: with Related Documents,* Neal Salisbury, ed. Boston: Bedford/St. Martin's Press, 1997.

Schultz, Eric B., and Michael Tougias. *King Philip's War: The History and Legacy of America's Forgotten Conflict*. Woodstock, Vt.: Countryman Press, 1999.

Vaughan, Alden. *New England Frontier: Puritans and Indians, 1620–1675*. 1965. 3rd Edition, Norman: University of Oklahoma Press, 1995.

WEB SITES

King Philip's War
http://www.bio.umass.edu/biology/conn.river/philip.html

National Park Service: The Great Swamp Fight
http://www.cr.nps.gov/history/online_books/regional_review/vol1-6f.htm

King Philip's War: Cultural, Gender, and Historical Implications
http://www.georgetown.edu/users/arsenauj/kpwtitle.html

Raid on Deerfield
http://1704.deerfield.history.museum/home.do

Wampanoag History
http://www.tolatsga.org/wampa.html

Picture Credits

Index

About the Contributors

Author **DANIEL R. MANDELL** is associate professor of history at Truman State University, Missouri, where he has taught early American and Native American history since 1999. He is the author of *Behind the Frontier: Indians in Eighteenth-Century Eastern Massachusetts*; the editor of the *Southern New England Treaties* and *Northern and Western New England Treaties* volumes in the series EARLY AMERICAN INDIAN DOCUMENTS: TREATIES AND LAWS; and author of the forthcoming *Tribe, Race, History: Indians in Southern New England, 1780–1880*. He has published many articles in edited collections, encyclopedias, and journals, including the *Journal of American History* and the *William and Mary Quarterly*, and has received research fellowships from the National Endowment for the Humanities and various research libraries.

Series editor **PAUL C. ROSIER** received his Ph.D. in American history from the University of Rochester in 1998. Dr. Rosier currently serves as assistant professor of history at Villanova University, where he teaches Native American history, the environmental history of America, history of American Capitalism, and world history. He is the author of *Rebirth of the Blackfeet Nation, 1912–1954* (2001) and *Native American Issues* (2003). His next book, on post-World War II Native American politics, will be published in 2008 by Harvard University Press. Dr. Rosier's work has also appeared in various journals, including the *Journal of American History*, the *American Indian Culture and Research Journal*, and the *Journal of American Ethnic History*.